Advance praise for *Why Would Feminists Trust th*

'*Why Would Feminists Trust the P* ...
ments taking place among radicals an ...
in feminist struggle: policing. Drawi ...
the front lines of resistance to policing, ... un provides clarity
and vision in tackling one of the most urgent issues of our time.'

Adam Elliott-Cooper, author of *Black Resistance to British Policing*

'The book we've been waiting for. Leah combines forensic
research with a rare and generous clarity of thought. I learned so
much about the history of policing and the pioneering attempts
to build something different and better in the future. This should
be required reading, especially for white women.'

Emily Kenway, author of *Who Cares*

'There has always been an ideological struggle between feminisms from below and feminisms of the status quo. While the
former is about freeing us all, the latter only seeks to free some
of us. Leah's vital intervention comes at a crucial time, where
violence against women is once again being weaponised to legitimise violence against racialised others. *Why Would Feminists
Trust the Police?* provides an essential antidote, and points us
towards a real feminist revolution.'

Shanice Octavia McBean, co-author of *Abolition Revolution*

'Meticulously deconstructs much feminist common sense about
safety, opening the way to brilliant abolitionist horizons that
might genuinely give the word meaning.'

Gracie Mae Bradley, co-author of *Against Borders*

'This unflinching history of mainstream British feminism's entanglements with the police deserves to be read by all feminists. Cowan tackles crucial questions, from why some suffrage campaigners eventually became fascists, to why some feminists demanded more police power after Sarah Everard was murdered by a serving police officer. She also explores the still-marginalised history of working-class, women-of-colour feminist organising which has sought transformation instead of control. This is essential reading to help us out of the quagmire in which gains for some women are still achieved at the expense of others.'

Alison Phipps, author of *Me, Not You: The Trouble with Mainstream Feminism*

'Leah writes urgently, persuasively and with a laser-like focus, using her expertise to carve open the limitations of carceral feminism in a British context, making it legible to those newly encountering it. "Timely" barely does justice to the necessity of this book right now.'

Paula Akpan, author of *When We Ruled: The Rise and Fall of Twelve African Queens and Warriors*

'A brilliant and much-needed book, which offers vital analysis of how British feminism became entangled in policing and why we urgently need a different approach ... This remarkable book offers important lessons for anyone seeking to end gender, racial, and economic violence. A beautifully written, carefully researched, and highly engaging read that interweaves historical analysis with cogent political insights.'

Sarah Lamble, professor of criminology and queer theory, Birkbeck

Why Would Feminists Trust the Police?

Why Would Feminists Trust the Police?

A Tangled History of Resistance and Complicity

Leah Cowan

VERSO

London • New York

First published by Verso 2024
© Leah Cowan 2024

1 3 5 7 9 10 8 6 4 2

Verso
UK: 6 Meard Street, London W1F 0EG
US: 388 Atlantic Avenue, Brooklyn, NY 11217
versobooks.com

Verso is the imprint of New Left Books

ISBN-13: 978-1-80429-303-4
ISBN-13: 978-1-80429-304-1 (UK EBK)
ISBN-13: 978-1-80429-305-8 (US EBK)

British Library Cataloguing in Publication Data
A catalogue record for this book is available from the British Library

Library of Congress Cataloging-in-Publication Data

Names: Cowan, Leah, author.
Title: Why would feminists trust the police? : a tangled history of
  resistance and complicity / Leah Cowan.
Description: London ; New York : Verso, 2024. | Includes bibliographical
  references and index.
Identifiers: LCCN 2024002442 (print) | LCCN 2024002443 (ebook) | ISBN
  9781804293034 (paperback) | ISBN 9781804293058 (ebk)
Subjects: LCSH: Police – Great Britain – Public opinion. | Discrimination in
  criminal justice administration – Great Britain. | Feminism – Great
  Britain. | Law enforcement – Moral and ethical aspects – Great Britain.
Classification: LCC HV8195.A2 C69 2024 (print) | LCC HV8195.A2 (ebook) |
  DDC 363.20941 – dc23/eng/20240206
LC record available at https://lccn.loc.gov/2024002442
LC ebook record available at https://lccn.loc.gov/2024002443

Typeset in Fournier by MJ & N Gavan, Truro, Cornwall
Printed in the UK by CPI Group (UK) Ltd, Croydon CR0 4YY

For Marvin Ogbonna-Godfrey,
thank you for your friendship

Contents

Acknowledgements

Thank you to Verso, and to the most brilliant editor Rosie Warren for your patience, insights, enthusiasm and expert steer – without you this book would not have come into existence. Thank you to Millie at United Agents for always championing my work.

Books do not spring fully formed from the heads of authors. This book is indebted to all the writers, thinkers, artists and organisers – especially the QTPOC – who have been building and struggling for abolition since day one. Thank you to everyone who I interviewed while researching this book, I truly appreciate the generosity of your time and that you were willing to share your experiences and analysis.

I'm very grateful to the individuals and communities who have held and supported me throughout the writing process. Endless thanks always to my parents and my sisters, who in so many ways made me who I am. I'm so grateful for my grandparents; at the time of writing, only my 102-year-old grandfather is still with us, but they are all present in my thoughts and ideas. Nobody is ever quite as impressed and enthused as a grandparent.

Thank you to all my colleagues and union comrades at Project 17 who do such brilliant work, and who provided cover so that I could take a short sabbatical to write.

The word 'friend' feels too flat and sterile for describing the people who lift me up, cook me meals, humour my obsessive scheduling, exchange podcast-length voicenotes with me, and let me lament to them over cocktails. My life's work is to offer you the same in return, and my heart is full to bursting with the joy of knowing you all. (You all know who you are; I'll just note that Ella and Esther: your companionship has made my life so rich.) Tatevik: your endless support is the greatest and best-wrapped gift, here's to the stanzas behind and the chapters ahead.

ACAB x

Introduction

Why Would Feminists Trust the Police?

Most Black people I know trust the police; they trust them to be exactly what they always have been: violent.

Derecka Purnell

Trust (verb): *To believe that someone is good and honest and will not harm you, or that something is safe and reliable.*

Cambridge English Dictionary

If you were a child in the 1990s, you could be forgiven for thinking that 'stranger danger' presented the most pressing threat to your smooth ascent into the new millennium. We were told, in frequent school assemblies and informational videos, that the people most likely to do us harm were shady, mysterious figures somewhere 'out there'. Local police officers would visit my school and inform the rows of cross-legged children that we must ready ourselves with an arsenal of responses to strangers: shouting loudly, kicking, running away, ideally towards a relative or friendly police officer who could protect us. Afterwards we would take turns to sit in the police car and run the lights.

These police visits to school were likely seen by the school administrators as wholesome and benign. In fact, 'stranger danger' narratives present an extremely skewed version of events: the vast majority of child abuse is perpetrated by someone known to the child. At the same time, the police, themselves strangers, were asking us to 'trust' them. They sought to form an idea in our young collective imagination that police are a force for good. However, these school visits wouldn't be my most formative interactions with law enforcement. Growing up, I became increasingly aware that security guards, border guards and police officers paid disproportionate attention to my family, whether we were browsing electronics shops, driving to visit our grandparents, or approaching passport control at the Channel Tunnel in Calais. These interactions were an early indicator to me that law enforcement and its agents were, at best, confused about their mission.

I remember clearly the news coverage when police shot and killed Jean Charles de Menezes in Stockwell tube station, after wrongly identifying him as being involved in the 7/7 London Tube and bus bombings. I had just turned sixteen, and was sitting my GCSEs at my cheerful but somewhat troubled high school that had failed multiple inspections and was chewing through headteachers at an alarming rate. The main image circulated by news outlets was taken from an ID card belonging to de Menezes, in which he looked solemnly into the camera. At the time I remember thinking that the 'mugshot-esque' photograph felt like an attempt to undermine his innocence even in death.

A flurry of reports suggested that de Menezes had acted suspiciously and had jumped over the Tube barrier to evade police. These allegations were soon revealed to be fabricated. I would later learn that the *Sunday Mirror* had attempted to smear the late de Menezes with a rape allegation.[1] As the following chapters explore, the use of 'women's safety' in attempted defence of state racism – de Menezes was Brazilian; the officers pursued him in the name of 'anti-terrorism' on the basis of a photograph of an Ethiopian man – is an age-old tactic that has no real investment in reducing harm in society.

Jean Charles de Menezes was neither the first nor the last victim of policing to hit national news in the 1990s. I was four years old when Joy Gardner was restrained, gagged and asphyxiated by border enforcement officers in her home in Hornsey, while her five-year-old son was held in an adjacent room, the same year that Stephen Lawrence was murdered by white racists at a bus stop in Eltham. I was nine years old when the inquiry into police failings to investigate Stephen's murder found the police to be 'institutionally racist'. I was twenty-two years old when Mark Duggan was shot by police in Tottenham, and, as in the wake of the murder of de Menezes, misinformation was spread by police and journalists, in this instance suggesting that Duggan had initiated the gunfire. As in the case of de Menezes, the media shared a head-and-shoulders photograph of Duggan grimacing at the camera – it was later revealed that the uncropped photograph shows Duggan holding a heart-shaped plaque at his daughter's funeral, contextualising that his face is contorted in grief. The circulation of these lies lit a touchpaper of civil unrest which spread across the country. The 'London riots' unfolded in August 2011, my first summer living in the city. In the mornings that followed evenings of unrest, I walked up Chalk Farm Road and saw that shops had barricaded their doors with furniture and a bench had been chucked through the window of a cycle chop. The London Metropolitan Police released 213 photographs of people 'wanted' for rioting, and encouraged members of the public to identify 'suspects'. This was a particularly alarming move given the risk of vigilante reprisals, as well as the Met Police's own history of using photographs of their 'targets' to justify violence in general – as happened in the case of de Menezes.

I was twenty-four when Christine Chase died of a heart attack while detained in Yarl's Wood Immigration Removal Centre. I was a member of a detention-visiting group at the time, and the person I was visiting in Yarl's Wood told me how the centre attempted to brush her death under the rug: 'They took away the other lady – her room-mate – they told her not to say anything … In the church, the pastor said that one of your friends has died, and said unfortunately we will pray for her, and that was it.'

The lives and bodies of Black girls and women appear to be particularly defilable and disposable in the eyes of the state. I was twenty-six when Sarah Reed was denied medical treatment and died while incarcerated in Holloway Prison. Sarah had previously been brutalised by Met Police constable James Kiddie in a shop on London's Regent Street, who dragged her by the hair across the floor, pressed her neck and repeatedly punched her in the head. I was thirty when a young student referred to as Child Q was strip-searched by Met Police officers at a school in East London. In the same year, sisters Bibaa Henry and Nicole Smallman were murdered in a park after attending a birthday picnic. Two officers who attended the scene, Deniz Jaffer and Jamie Lewis, took 'selfies' with the sisters' bodies, and shared them in a WhatsApp group with other police officers.

I was thirty-one when, a year later, Sarah Everard was abducted, raped and murdered by police officer Wayne Couzens. Couzens was given a life sentence; this was the first time someone who had murdered one adult outside the context of a 'terrorist' attack (by the court's own framing) was handed such a sentence. In court, the barrister defending Couzens – Jim Sturman QC – attempted to push into the background the critical importance of Couzens being a police officer, claiming, 'Whilst this may well be considered by the public and the court to be a case of equal seriousness to a political, religious, or ideological murder, it is not such an offence.' Sturman noted that when Couzens murdered Sarah, he was 'a police officer, albeit off duty in half uniform'.[2] The emphasis on Couzens being 'off duty' and the bizarre concept of 'half uniform' – Couzens used his police ID and handcuffs to detain Sarah, and utilised his police belt to strangle her – was an attempt by Sturman to divorce Couzens from his job as a police officer, as he knew this would be an aggravating factor in the length of his sentence. Yet the violence Couzens perpetrated was police violence *and* business as usual: his ability to coerce and Sarah's inability to deny his instructions were enabled because of his role as a police officer. At a vigil held in the park where Sarah was abducted, police officers turned up and brutalised those who had gathered to pay respects to her memory.

Police violence is a consistent component of life in Britain. So is police incompetence, especially in cases of gender-based violence (GBV). For example, police failed to investigate fourteen similar reports by women of 'strange incidents' dating back to 2002, some including sexual assault, after taking a taxi driven by black cab driver John Worboys late at night in central London. The women described remarkably comparable experiences: a cab driver claiming to have won the lottery, offering a spiked glass of champagne to his customer, who falls unconscious and is then sexually assaulted. The police were unreactive to these reports, and it is thought that Warboys assaulted over 100 women.[3] The police also failed to do their jobs in the murder case of Valerie Forde and her daughter Real-Jahzara, who were killed in 2014 by Forde's ex-partner despite her reporting his threats to the police. Tellingly, the ex-partner's threats that he would burn down her house with Forde inside were logged by the police as a 'threat to property', rather than a threat to life.[4] In 2017, Dorset police also missed opportunities to safeguard nineteen-year-old Gaia Pope, who had contacted them to make an appointment to report online sexual harassment, in a state of an acute mental health crisis, hours before she went missing. Police logs noted that panicked calls from her relatives when she went missing were 'taking the piss'. She was later found dead.[5]

Public opinion polls conducted by YouGov in 2021 found that when people in Britain were asked about the general 'concept' of the police, the majority of people sampled thought they were doing a 'good job'. However, when asked to consider the reality of policing – for example, how effective police actually were in their local area, around half of respondents expressed low or no confidence in the police. Office of National Statistics (ONS) data likewise show that public confidence in the police declined from about 62 per cent expressing confidence in 2017–18, to 55 per cent in 2019–20.[6] When YouGov asked about the London Metropolitan Police in particular (whose current strategy states that its vision is 'for the Met to be the most trusted police service in the world'[7]), trust rapidly declined, particularly among people aged eighteen to twenty-four.[8] This could be attributed to the fact that the actions of the Met Police have been widely communicated in popular media: it was the Met Police who were found to be 'institutionally racist' in their response (or lack thereof) to the racist murder of Stephen Lawrence in 1993. It was during a Met Police raid in 2011 that reggae star Smiley Culture died from a stab wound. It was two Met Police officers who posed for selfies alongside the bodies of Nicole Smallman and Bibaa Henry, and it was a Met Police officer who used COVID-19 legislation to murder Sarah Everard.

The paradox of criminal legal solutions for violence

The criminal-legal system was not set up to reduce harm in society, but to protect private property and the interests of capital and 'imperial expansion' – the practice of a state growing its power and domination through military and colonial expeditions in other regions. The law functions as a key component of capitalism, meaning that it upholds a system where the priorities of powerful and wealthy elites are elevated above the lives of everyday people. We see this demonstrated in the types of 'crime' that the law recognises, and the communities it places most frequently in its crosshairs – it is a crime to 'steal' formula milk you cannot afford to feed your hungry baby, but not a crime to cover high-rise buildings in highly combustible cladding.

In the 1980s, scholar and radical theorist Cedric Robinson described the dominant economic system as 'racial capitalism'. He pointed out its reliance upon relationships of inequality between human groups.[9] Academic Jodi Melamed fleshes out how capitalism is inherently racialised, in that it 'creates fictions of differing human capacities', historically along lines of race within a system of class. This has direct implications for the formation and implementation of legal systems that are invested in keeping these fictions alive. In this context, proposing police and prisons as a solution to feminist issues constitutes – depending on your outlook – something between an 'act of bad faith' and a wilful attempt to preclude vast swathes of people from the possibility of safety or justice.[10]

When Sarah Everard was murdered by police officer Wayne Couzens, some organisations working in the UK's GBV sector (also known as the 'women's sector') intensified calls to bring acts of 'misogyny' into the hate crime framework.[11] The existing hate crime framework allows for the possibility of aggravated (harsher) sentences for lawbreaking which demonstrates or is motivated by hostility based on race, religion, disability, sexuality or transgender identity. The proposal put forward by some factions of the GBV sector is to include misogyny in the hate crime framework on the basis that 'including misogyny in hate crime law would send a message to the public and to the police that women's safety matters'.[12] That these organisations proposed to use law enforcement and the police to protect women from misogyny *in response to a woman being murdered by a police officer* begs the question: is there any problem to which these organisations would not suggest the solution of more laws and tougher sentences?

Hate crime policies fail to hold accountable those who are responsible for driving inequality and violence in society, such as governments and corporations who create and exacerbate financial crises, and who spew and whip up abusive and divisive rhetoric on mass media platforms. Calls for the expansion of hate crime frameworks are a prime example of what American sociologist Elizabeth Bernstein termed 'carceral feminism' in the late 2000s. The term has increasingly been used in the past decade or so to describe pro-police and prison-forward approaches to 'feminist issues'. 'Carceral feminists' are those who seek 'social remedies through criminal justice interventions rather than through a redistributive welfare state', and which 'locate social problems in deviant individuals' rather than in the mainstream institutions that harm them.[13] This carceral feminist approach turns away from addressing root and structural causes of harm, and towards atomising issues down to individuals who can be punished and socially abandoned, one by one.

The loudest voices in the so-called women's sector in Britain have for many years been pushing for more prosecutions and convictions of people who perpetrate rape. Significant amounts of funding are channelled into the collection and review of data on prosecutions for sexual violence, rates of which are the lowest since records began. While the motivation for these efforts may be about improving support for survivors, many seek to create specialist police officers to take statements in rape cases, and envisage rape prosecution as being a specialist and 'well-rewarded' career route within the criminal-legal system.[14] Consequently, this campaigning around rape prosecutions directly supports the channelling of more funds and feminist energies into the police, the courts and the judiciary – a more 'winnable' victory in the context of a government that prioritises law and order over social care and meaningful justice.

Carceral feminism also manifests as the development of part-nerships – both financial and operational – between GBV services and government departments such as the Ministry of Justice and the Home Office. These same government departments, in the name of gender equality, also open women's prisons, transgender prison wings and women-only immigration detention centres. Carceral feminism encapsulates a reliance on policing, sentenc-ing, probation, prisons, immigration enforcement and other oppressive systems as a desirable response to gender-based harm and violence.

The implicit message here is that the state and its agents *can* save us; that they can play a leading role in our liberated futures, if only they could be properly resourced and trained, and would step up to the plate. Carceral feminism encourages us to trust the institution of the criminal-legal system to keep watch as we march towards liberation – a logic which is divorced from reality. Where police action on 'crime' is 'successful', the resultant prosecutions and prison sentences do little more than fuel inequality. As a grass-roots organiser explained to me, 'There are some, like, rich white women who could put a man in jail if they got sexually assaulted, which might feel good for them. I don't want to take that away from them, but it's not making anyone else any safer, and the chance of them being able to do that is only [likely] if the man actually has less institutional or structural power than she does.'

Very rarely does the criminal-legal system pursue figures with economic and institutional power, such as Jimmy Savile, who used his position as a DJ and radio host to abuse hundreds of children and young people and evaded any criminal-legal punishment; or Prince Andrew, who faced allegations of involvement in sex trafficking yet did not face any criminal repercussions; or Wayne Couzens, who prior to murdering Sarah Everard was nicknamed 'the Rapist' by his police colleagues, who didn't see fit to escalate their concerns. Most commonly, the people who face both the everyday violence of policing and the full force of the law are working-class and marginalised people who have been simultaneously targeted and abandoned by the state.

A few bad apples and a broken system

Contrary to popular opinion, in general, police time is not spent catching serial killers and solving mysteries: a 2020 report by police watchdogs suggests that up to 80 per cent of police work is not actually dedicated towards 'crime'.[15] The police are paid to carry out work that we might not even imagine as being within their remit, such as escorting people on probation to appointments, and helping people apply for benefits. In addition, police forces spend time developing partnerships with other agencies such as immigration enforcement, domestic abuse charities, local authorities and mental healthcare provision, which expands their reach into every aspect of daily life, enabling them to gather 'intelligence' from a huge range of public bodies.

There are two interrelated paradigms underlining feminist pro-police stances. These are ways of (partially) grappling with (some of) the violence of the police, without conceding the idea that the police as an institution must be abolished wholesale. The first is the paradigm of the 'broken system': this is the idea that police and prisons have the potential to provide a useful function in addressing GBV and feminist issues, but that there is something 'broken' or maligned about their current operations. The narrative goes: if only the system could be fixed, the otherwise competent police would be able to protect (some) women better.

Feminists using the 'broken system' analysis typically make demands that police forces' crime-fighting skills should be improved, that officers should 'do their job properly' and that legal mechanisms should be put in place to hold the police accountable when they fall short.[16] Reforms such as police training (on anti-racism, mental health, 'violence against women and girls', equality and inclusion, 'unconscious bias' and so on[17]) or diversity recruitment drives might appear like quite positive or benign activities. In fact, these reforms work to make an inherently violent system more robust and resilient to critique.

New criminal-legal legislation and policies, which are assumed to have both punitive and deterrent abilities, often bring an expectation that police trained on the newly criminalised topic will be better able to identify perpetrators and assist victims. When the Serious Crime Act 2015 created a new offence of coercive control in a context of domestic abuse, the charity Safe-Lives helped to create the 'Domestic Abuse Matters' training that aimed to 'begin a cultural change in policing when responding to controlling and coercive behaviour by putting the voice of the victim at the centre'.[18] The national charity Women's Aid is also licensed to deliver this training course, which 'ensures that frontline officers and staff understand the impacts of domestic abuse and why protective measures can be life-saving'.[19] New offences generally mean more funding being channelled into the police and the agencies that are willing to be complicit in their operations. In the run-up to economic abuse being recognised as a form of GBV in the Domestic Abuse Act 2021, funding was granted by the Home Office to develop more police training.[20]

Despite good intentions, training individuals within an inherently violent institution won't lead to the diffusion of non-violent praxis throughout the force. As academic Betsy Stanko (who previously worked in the Mayor's Office for Policing and Crime in London) writes, 'Police training is largely hermetically sealed within the core culture of policing, one that continues to be criticised for its macho culture, lack of diversity and command and control ethos.'[21] Training materials are largely devised and reviewed internally, and workshops are typically delivered by officers who are 'burnt out' and taking a rest from frontline work.

Policing methods and processes taught in training are often decided based on understandings of 'how things are done around here', and approaches are resistant to external or evidence-based input.[22] In summary, Stanko describes police training as a mystical 'black box'.

I spoke with a worker from the GBV sector, who also shared her frustration with the reliance on 'police training' as a solution to an inherently violent system. She makes reference to the police taking photographs of themselves with the bodies of Nicole Smallman and Bibaa Henry: 'One of the things that really makes me quite upset is when the reaction is: "well, let's just train police". Because this has been going on for decades … why did the police need to be trained to not take selfies? … because you and I know it's not something we should do, ever.'

Information gleaned on trainings is merely absorbed and integrated into the unspoken objective of the police, becoming further arsenal to use against the marginalised communities they largely interact with. I spoke with Lucy McKay from INQUEST, a charity that provides expertise on state-related deaths to bereaved families and their lawyers, and she explained some of the impacts of training the police. She outlined how training police on mental health has had the consequence of equipping them with a larger portfolio of excuses that can be leveraged when somebody dies after police contact. A range of symptoms and behaviours such as being fearful, agitated or aggressive have been grouped together and termed 'acute behavioural disturbance' (ABD) or 'excited delirium'. McKay explained how describing someone's behaviour using the umbrella term ABD has been utilised as a smokescreen for their murder by police: 'What's supposed to happen is, it's supposed to be a medical emergency and you're supposed to respond by contacting an ambulance, as you shouldn't restrain someone who's exhibiting these symptoms. But what actually happens is often [the police] do exactly the same things that they would have done [without mental health training]. But then at the end, they go: "Oh, they had ABD, didn't they?" And then that's almost the excuse for why they died.'

Police training does not keep us safe. It shunts more funding into the police, and the co-production of training by charities and non-profit organisations diverts their resources and energy away from the critical work of directly supporting communities who are most affected by police encounters.

The second, sometimes simultaneously unleashed, paradigm is that of the 'bad apple' or 'lone wolf'. This approach tends to condemn the actions of a specific police officer or group of officers, as divorced from the purpose and functioning of the police as a whole – which is otherwise understood to be a crucial and effective institution, although sometimes system glitches have enabled bad apples to fester on the branch. When Wayne Couzens murdered Sarah Everard, the government was quick to reach for the paradigm of the 'bad apple', with then Home Secretary Priti Patel noting that 'the professionalism and conduct I have witnessed through my own engagement with the police since Sarah's disappearance has reminded me that the vast majority of police officers serve with the utmost integrity and represent the very best of public service'.[23] The police announced that plain clothes officers would no longer be deployed alone,[24] suggesting that the toxicity of bad apples could be diluted if surrounded by enough shiny red good ones, and that the police would somehow hold each other accountable.

Often such 'bad apple' incidents involve extreme physical harm or murder by police. Pro-police logics understand these actions as being divorced from the police's everyday function; an officer caught up in a high-profile case of 'police brutality' might be seen as acting above and beyond their job description in a way that is generally recognised as violent. The 'lone wolf' paradigm concludes that these officers are like a badly decayed tooth in an otherwise healthy mouth: they are beyond repair and must be extracted. Long, harsh prison sentences are presented as the preferable solution.

Both paradigms are red herrings. They work to gloss over long histories and current realities. The police are simply not suitable for intervening in situations of harm, nor do they prevent harm from happening in the first place. The 'broken system' and the 'bad apple' are misplaced attempts to make sense of the inherent harms of policing. In more progressive spaces where there is typically less enthusiastic support for policing and prisons, these 'lone wolf' actions might be described as acts of 'police violence' or 'police brutality'. I spoke with Koshka Duff, a lecturer in social and political philosophy at the University of Nottingham, about the way police violence is normalised. They explained to me that police 'brutality' in many ways represents business as usual: 'The question that is often asked about some kind of troubling feature or aspect of policing is: is it excessive? Is it police brutality? Or is it actually essential to modern policing? Is it police just doing their jobs? My analysis is that it can be both.'

Duff's reflections encourage us to consider how social acceptance of 'everyday' policing requires the normalising and legitimising of violence. We might question what types of violence are deemed 'lawful', and who can 'get away' with harassing and brutalising people because their actions are legally sanctioned.

What is trustworthy about police in England?

Policing by consent is an instruction which was given to the first Metropolitan Police officers in 1829 and relied on the idea that if police applied the law fairly and with 'minimal force', acted with transparency, and provided opportunities for the public to provide feedback on local policing, the public would not seek to disrupt them in their duties. A Home Office freedom of information (FOI) release in 2012 expands on this idea, describing Britain's 'policing by consent' approach as 'unique throughout the world' as it is 'derived not from fear but almost exclusively from public co-operation'.[25] This tidy definition overlooks the fact that coercion in a context of fear can look very much like co-operation. When the alternative to 'co-operation' is to encounter the criminal-legal system, 'consent' cannot freely be given. After all, the government's own definition of coercive control – 'a purposeful pattern of incidents that occur over time in order for one individual to exert power, control or coercion over another'[26] – is also an accurate description of policing.

In Britain, this idea of policing by consent pushes a narrative that there is something specific about *British* police that makes them particularly trustworthy, unlike other police forces who are prone to corruption and excessive use of force. This is partially rooted in a centuries-old idea that Britain is morally exceptional in its values of democracy, tolerance, liberty and the rule of law (or so the Department for Education would have us believe[27]). These values are sculpted reactively, posed as mirror opposites to the values that other countries (former colonies in particular) supposedly lack: in 2005 then chancellor Gordon Brown orated, 'The days of Britain having to apologise for its colonial history are over ... We should talk, and rightly so, about British values that are enduring, because they stand for some of the greatest ideas in history.' Brown alludes to this idea that we 'do things differently' over here. This narrativising around Britain spear-heading ideas of equality and democracy as part of the colonial project leads directly to the myth of 'policing by consent', which is overtly a communications exercise seeking to avoid popular resistance to policing.

A so-called feminist collaboration with the police requires glossing over long, interlinked, globe-spanning histories of working-class resistance by marginalised communities to the oppression honed and exported by Britain. Encounters between groups organising around social, economic and anti-colonial justice, and the British 'police' in a variety of forms, have con-sistently been astronomically violent. British policing tactics have always been skill-shared across its global imperial portfolio, including through the transfer of officers between different colo-nial outposts. For example, in 1920 the Royal Irish Constabulary recruited British ex-soldiers who had fought in the First World War to provide police back-up during the Irish War of Inde-pendence. These barely trained officers, dubbed the 'Black and Tans' due to their cobbled-together mismatching uniforms, were notoriously violent and carried out sexual assaults and forced head-shearing of Irish women from Republican families in particular.[28]

A year or so later, Winston Churchill created the British Gendarmerie in Palestine. He tasked this police force with pro-tecting the settlers who were arriving and commandeering land and property in British-occupied Palestine: a precursor to the 1948 Nakba, which marks the violent formation of the state of Israel through ongoing occupation of land and displacement of Palestinians. The majority of the British Gendarmerie in

Palestine were recruited directly from the Royal Irish Constabulary, including from the Black and Tans, who would soon be out of a job as talks moved towards the partition of Ireland.[29] British police in Palestine used tactics developed in Ireland to assist and facilitate the ongoing brutalisation and expropriation carried out by the state of Israel. When Britain retreated from occupied Palestine as the Nakba unfolded in 1948, its counterinsurgency methods developed in Palestine were then exported to Malaya (now Malaysia), where pro-independence communists were leading an insurgency against British colonial rule.

The violence of policing in a context of colonialism dovetails with recent history and the continuing reality of police violence against our communities. In 2022, Metropolitan Police in the London Borough of Hackney, where I live, welcomed a police delegation from Israel, and took them on a joint patrol of the area.[30] Just one week prior, Israeli forces had shot and killed Al Jazeera journalist Shireen Abu Akleh, and Israeli police had attacked mourners at her funeral. At a vigil I joined outside Stoke Newington Police Station to protest the joint patrol, an academic stepped up to speak. They explained that the presence of Israeli police in Hackney was further evidence that enforcement tactics 'circulate between police and traverse boundaries between the police and military'. This long-standing strategic terrorism meted out by police does not leave space for 'trust'. Trust is not found in the dynamic between an agent of the state tasked with maintaining a framework of oppression refined over centuries, and those whom the state is oppressing.

A simple story of victims, villains and heroes

Carceral feminism is premised upon a limited vision of *who* is entitled to safety, justice and liberation; who needs saving; and who is beyond redemption. Carceral responses to feminist issues on the whole employ binary understandings of gender and are primarily invested in the protection of cisgender women and their freedom from 'male' violence. This concentration on 'male' violence against women obfuscates harms experienced within, for example, queer relationships or as enacted by parents of any gender against children, or by state agents of any gender against individuals and communities. It reduces issues of structural inequality to one of interpersonal disputes – a bitter war between men and women with a clear-cut villain and a straightforward victim. Carceral feminism's simplistic men-versus-women battle also overlooks the experiences of people who are racialised; carceral feminists have nothing to say about the racism of the state or the police, or about the racism of individual white women.

The carceral feminist 'white saviour' impulse also frequently dovetails with moves to limit the economic options of sex workers. Carceral feminist arguments against sex work coalesce with the delegitimisation by the state of certain types of ostensibly gendered and racialised precarious labour – including carers, cleaners, hotel workers and domestic workers, among others – with these workers often denied police 'protection' and instead subjected to harassment and abuse, taken into custody by police and other state agents such as border enforcement. In the UK, sex work is criminalised, and so when workers face abuse in their workplaces they have to assess the negligible benefits of reporting to the same state agents who are tasked with upholding laws against their very livelihoods. Similarly, since 2012, domestic workers who travel to the UK for employment on 'tied visas' are not able to renew their visas if they change employers, and for a number of years weren't allowed to change employers at all. This effectively obliges workers in abusive situations (which are more commonly experienced than not[31]) to remain with those employers, or risk facing immigration enforcement action.[32] The possibility of protection by police evaporates in these spaces. It is the very threat of action *by* agents of the law here which pushes workers into situations that are unsafe.

In moments of crisis and high risk, survivors who are racialised or otherwise marginalised have to weigh up the potential harm of a police intervention (to themselves and to the person who is being violent), versus the harm of no intervention at all. Reporting abuse perpetrated by people within our own communities also requires these same considerations: against the outcome of not reporting abuse, survivors balance the possible harm caused by fanning the flames of centuries-old racist stereotypes that frame racialised men, and also women, as aggressive and predatory. Furthermore, the state's ability to destabilise a person of colour's right to remain in the country continues to grow. Migrant communities have always been wary of police contact due to well-founded fears of potential immigration enforcement action, and the state's ability to deport, arrest and harass people of colour is increasing.

Carceral feminism's commitment to police and prisons also ignores the inherent danger that the police represent for people who are in mental health crisis or who are neurodivergent. An investigation conducted by *HUCK* magazine revealed that in the past decade, just under half of the people who died during or following police custody had 'known mental health concerns'.[33]

I spoke to Janey Starling, director of feminist organisation Level Up, about police responses to crisis incidents, and she explained that 'when there is someone in mental health distress, or [there's] a domestic abuse incident, or there's sexual harassment you need something to defuse and de-escalate it. It's never going to be the police. It's literally not what they're there for ... When you see someone who's clearly in psychological distress, obviously don't call the police!'

Furthermore, policing and prisons themselves create and compound mental health issues and ableism. As Micha Frazer-Carroll, author of *Mad World: The Politics of Mental Health*, tells me, 'If you believe in police and prisons as legitimate interventions into societal problems, then you essentially are okay with the mass production of mental distress.' Micha describes prisons as 'environments that are strategically designed to make people miserable. To make people mad'. Likewise, policing led by racial profiling specifically has been shown to result in depression, anxiety and hypervigilance for marginalised communities who are targeted by this form of surveillance and harassment.[34]

The police do not deliver us from harm; they entrench it. It is only by addressing violence as perpetrated across society and by the state that we can understand violence as a consistent component of the system of racial capitalism we live in – a system that is reliant upon gender-based violence, among other harms, to maintain a landscape of inequality. The solutions proposed by tackling this system of harm at its root are more robust, more creative, more tangible and more various than the narrow confines of the criminal-punishment system: this book is one effort to think about why we urgently need to continue moving in this direction, and away from carceral thinking and systems.

Why Would Feminists Trust the Police? seeks to understand how we got here: why have feminists trusted the police and the law to make women safe? Crucially, if they are wrong to do so, what is the alternative? How did mainstream British feminism arrive at its current carceral approach? What were the contributing factors and political basis for the deployment of tactics that are reliant upon the criminal-punishment system? The chapters that follow examine British feminism's complicated and contradictory relationship with policing. This history includes contention between carceral feminist approaches and the work of communities of thinkers, organisers and healers who have always encountered the violence of the state as a key player within racial capitalism.

I do not claim to present a full, comprehensive account of British feminisms and their relationship with the police. To quote Black feminist writer and organiser Lola Olufemi, 'Feminist histories are unwieldy; they cannot and should not be neatly presented.'[35] In my analysis I have sought to learn from and build alongside the writings and work of working-class organisers, while acknowledging that I have much more to learn and reflect upon beyond the scope of this research period. This work is also heavily weighted towards the histories of feminism in England, and London in particular. The specific contexts of feminist and anti-racist resistance in Wales, Scotland and Ireland must not be folded into broad generalisations; the nature of England's relationship with these nations, and Ireland in particular, charts its own course of oppression by police agents – and writers, thinkers and organisers in these locations offer more pertinent and useful analysis than mine.

In this book I present threads of ideas, analysis and provocations, which are based on interviews and research. I walk with and alongside ideas, linked experiences, and fragments of history that are buffeted on a wind that urges us forwards. These threads mesh together, providing a partial tapestry which I hope will be discussed, rent apart and built on. This work is indebted to the Black feminist and abolitionist thinkers, writers and organisers who have taught me (knowingly or otherwise), and gone before me. My perspective on this topic is informed by organising in London-based anti-border and feminist movements, alongside working in the British charity sector in what is referred to as the 'migrants' rights' and the 'women's' sectors for over a decade. In researching this book, my analysis was also informed by interviews I conducted with people thinking, working and organising in these spaces, including survivors of GBV and state violence in Britain; organisers and founding members of grass-roots groups working on issues of state violence and gender-based violence; academics researching police, borders and carceral structures in Britain; and workers from support and advocacy services for survivors of gender-based violence. I am thankful for, and humbled by, the generosity and openness of those who took time to speak to me.

I've dedicated some time in this introduction to exploring the paradox of placing trust in police to solve issues of harm in society, despite a wealth of evidence that they are at best unable to solve harm, and at worst directly perpetrate it. The book which follows doesn't concern itself with the question of whether the continued validation, funding and expansion of prisons and police brings us closer to a liberated future. For those looking for more detail on the downfalls and dangers of the carceral system more broadly, I have provided a reading list at the back of this book. I take as a starting point the position that carceral feminism is a dominant (but, crucially, ineffective) anti-violence strategy in segments of British feminist movements. The chapters that follow will examine the development of carceral feminist logic and activity in Britain, which relies upon and provides fuel to the police. The book also tracks its opposite: the feminist organising and resistance that has always opposed policing and prisons. Claiming and building on this tradition is what leads us towards abolitionist futures.

1

False Histories in the Shadow of the Empire

What is placed in or left out of the archive is a political act, dictated by the archivist.

Carmen Maria Machado

Queer feminists must become comfortable positioning some feminists – even queer ones – as their enemies.

Sophie Lewis and Asa Seresin

In a photograph from 1910 – which at the time of writing is on display at the Museum of London – suffragette Ada Wright is lying on the ground after being struck by an officer, while a policeman in a long coat and a helmet looms over her motionless body. In another photograph from 1914, suffragette Emmeline Pankhurst is grabbed around her middle by a burly police officer and lifted up so that her well-shod feet are dangling in mid-air. A third photograph from the museum's collection depicts a bustling crowd of officers, and in the foreground a neatly dressed woman in a long coat, hat and patent shoes is clamped around a policeman's baton with a determined grimace on her face, earnestly holding on as he attempts to tug it away. These images speak to the combative approach that police adopted in response to campaigns for (some) women to have the right to vote. Indeed, some of the most enduring images of nineteenth-century feminist activism are of women in smart skirts and jackets being roughed up by agents of the state. Beyond the frames of these images, protestors were facing further violence and brutality through arrests, sexual assaults, imprisonment and force-feeding. As we expand our viewfinder further still, we find that the storyboard of feminism in Britain, which so often focuses on particular women taking particular types of action, is full of layers, pivots and causalities that point to a much more complex web of actors and ideas.

According to most historical records and mainstream narratives, the British feminist 'movement' has always been fronted by relatively wealthy white English women who appear to set the agenda of feminist work, while work which sits outside their agenda goes on behind the scenes nonetheless. This multi-layered feminist history raises the question, who do we mean when we say 'feminists'? This isn't just a historical question; there are continuing debates about who can claim to be a 'real' feminist. Yet attempts to gatekeep the moniker 'feminist' are likely to be a fruitless mission, a pursuit that is uninspiring and unproductive for all involved. Feminism as a broad school of thought rooted in history encapsulates a host of actors and activities with wildly differing objectives. Attempting to sweep the less commendable activities and theoretical foundations of British feminism under the carpet does us no favours.[1] This book argues that part of the reason for the continued feminist alliance with the police is the way that feminism tries to tidy up its own lineage and history without learning from the past.

Under and beyond the waves

The first 'wave' of feminism began in Europe and North America in the nineteenth century, so the story goes, and was focused on property rights and the right to vote (or 'suffrage'). The second 'wave' in the 1960s and 1970s, we're told, sought to reconfigure women's role in the home and in public spheres, including reproductive rights. The third 'wave' in the late 1990s is defined by the 'feminist sex wars', with pornography and sex work (and the condemnation of both) emerging as divisive issues.[2] A potential 'fourth wave' of feminism emerged in the 2010s. This wave was characterised by the use of the internet as a site of organising and activism, focusing on criminal-legal responses to rape culture, media sexism and sexual harassment in public spaces, university campuses and the workplace, as well as grappling with the limitations of the movement as we inherited it, via an 'intersectional' analysis. This era of feminism is undergirded by the period of economic downturn which began with the 2008 financial crisis and unfolded with the decade of 'austerity' that followed.

The wave analogy is a shorthand that shines light on a fragment of feminist genealogy, but it's an oversimplification. It starts the clock on resistance to British patriarchy with the actions of white women on British soil. This is an incomplete story which suggests that the feminist activity of women of colour and racialised communities arriving from the 1950s onwards was mystically self-igniting, and ignores long histories of struggle against social and economic depression in contexts of colonialism, as well as connections between those struggles and internationalist movements for justice. Reflecting on the work of writer and scholar Sara Ahmed, academic Heidi Safia Mirza instead offers an alternative of 'lifelines' that are thrown to successive generations by Black British feminism.[3] The idea that women's organising against British oppression 'began' with a first wave of activity as late as the nineteenth century over-looks organising that predates this era, including anti-colonial struggles for justice against British imperial patriarchy. These struggles set the tone and tenor of the feminist organising that follows centuries later when women from colonised countries travel to the hub of the empire. If we pivot our understanding of resistance away from feminist activities that are most photo-graphed and best documented, and towards organising which centres justice and freedom from patriarchal structures in a context of racial capitalism, our vision of the movement takes on a much vaster, more vibrant and more liberatory aspect. The way in which we understand the past – especially in terms of whose resistance matters – influences our perspective on strug-gles in the present.

Pre-dating the supposed 'first wave' are the revolts by enslaved women, and women's involvement in anti-colonial resistance across the British Empire. According to historian Rebecca Hall, slave ships' logs show that organised resistance against slave traders was more likely to occur on ships that held higher numbers of women.[4] In eighteenth-century Jamaica, Nanny of the Maroons organised a community of people who had escaped slavery, and led a vicious guerrilla war against the colonial British authorities. The focus of these struggles was around 'property' – a key objective of first-wave feminism – but liberation *from* the property ledgers of white colonialists, rather than concerns around how to acquire and inherit land and assets. Before the nineteenth century dawned, women also played a key role in the Haitian revolution, including Marie-Jeanne Lamartinière, who fought in a man's uniform; Catherine Flon, a nurse and seamstress who in oral tradition is said to have sewn the first Haitian flag;[5] and Cécile Fatiman, a vodou priestess who led a ritual that sparked the revolution.[6] In European-settled North America, slave-catching patrols (the predecessors of the police) also met with resistance from people who had escaped plantations, and who strategised to evade recapture.[7]

Sixty years after Nanny's death and back in the hub of the empire, Mary Wollstonecraft pens *A Vindication of the Rights of Woman*.[8] Wollstonecraft makes liberal reference to 'slavery' in this text – as an analogy for white women's struggles in Britain. Wollstonecraft writes that women are 'slaves to their bodies', and decries the 'specious slavery that chains the very soul of woman, keeping her for ever under the bondage of ignorance': the 'slavery of marriage'. She was not alone in using this rhetoric. Philosopher John Stuart Mill, in his 1869 essay 'The Subjection of Women', wrote that 'no slave is a slave to the same lengths, and in so full a sense of the word, as a wife is'.[9] He qualified this with his claim that enslaved Black women have times when they are 'off duty', whereas wives do not. Of course, enslaved Black women were prohibited from being wives at all, but were instead viewed as breeding machines who were commonly beaten and raped by slave-owners – details that Mill overlooks. The slave-owners' wives, meanwhile, were protected from the dehumanisation meted out to enslaved women by virtue of their elevated position within the racial and class hierarchy.

Wollstonecraft and those who argued for (some) women's

suffrage in the decades that followed continued to draw these tenuous comparisons between the enslavement of people from African countries, and the position of women in English society. Yet, across the Atlantic, Black women were wearing actual shackles; women who were oppressed due to gender inequality but were *also* enslaved by the British state fell outside Wollstonecraft's analogy. Fundamental here is that mainstream British feminism kick-starts a pattern that will replicate throughout the centuries that follow: that of always having its boot on the neck of women who do not have access to roles of respectability within the framework of the state, and who are therefore kept from the category of womanhood which mainstream feminist activity seeks to protect.

Where white women *were* writing critically about transatlantic slavery, the arguments being made for abolition became increasingly counterproductive. White women in Britain, like their US counterparts, were quick to draw parallels between the oppression of enslaved women and their own lesser rank in the sociopolitical hierarchy, so much so that American abolitionist Frederick Douglass would comment, 'When the true history of the antislavery cause should be written, women will occupy a large space in its pages; for the cause of the slave has been peculiarly women's cause.'[10] The representation by white women of enslaved women as passive victims without agency provided fuel to British colonial representations of people from African countries as the 'child races'.[11] For example, in an anonymous abolitionist pamphlet entitled *A Dialogue between a Well-Wisher and a Friend to the Slaves in the British Colonies by a Lady*, the authors describe enslaved women as 'poor creatures', remarking that for slave-owners, enslaved people are 'as much his duty to take care of as it is to take care of his own children'.[12]

Journalist and researcher Ruhi Khan notes that the narrative overlap between British anti-slavery efforts and its women's suffrage movements were 'instrumental in white western bourgeois women's demand for political rights and freedom'.[13] Through this infantilisation of enslaved women on faraway plantations, we also see the crystallisation of the 'victim–perpetrator' binary which forms the bedrock of carceral feminist attitudes into the twenty-first century. While seeking to identify the power dynamics which enable individual acts of abuse, the deployment of this binary – almost presenting violence as inevitable due to the inherent powerlessness of the victim – fails to address root causes of systematic and structural forms of violence. This type of 'abolitionism' seeks to illegalise only the symptoms of structural inequality, without upsetting its fundamental basis.

In the same era, campaigns in the US to secure women's suffrage were being boosted by indignation that Black men might get the right to vote before the white women who oversaw their enslavement. In a feminist newspaper, one outraged contributor writes, 'If educated women are not as fit to decide who shall be the rulers of this country, as "field hands," then where's the use of culture, or any brain at all? One might as well have been "born on the plantation".'[14] Similarly, nineteenth-century women's rights activist Elizabeth Cady Stanton, who initially influenced Frederick Douglass to support the movement for women's suffrage, would later comment when asked if she would support the enfranchisement of Black men before white women, 'I would not trust him with all my rights; degraded, oppressed himself, he would be more despotic with the governing power than even our Saxon rulers are.'[15] Time and time again, we will observe this – opening the door to certain privileges for an elite group of white women, while closing it swiftly behind them to prevent anyone else from enjoying those same liberties – to be the stumbling block of the mainstream feminist movement in Britain, and a seamless pathway into carceral logics.

Feminist tactics in Victorian Britain: for empire and for suffrage

Around the turn of the twentieth century, women in Britain began organising around two topics that are critical to our understanding of carceral feminism in the present day: support for the empire, and the issue of 'suffrage' – the right to vote in elections. In fact, these two issues would become intrinsically linked. Support for empire necessarily championed the expansion of the state and its power, including the use of military and police agents to control and repress anti-colonial uprisings. Equally, the campaign for suffrage leveraged pro-empire ideas, with self-identifying suffragist 'mothers of the race' arguing that women's involvement in parliamentary matters – particularly on issues relating to health and social care – was crucial in enabling the advancement of a strong and healthy 'race' in Britain.

Such arguments are premised upon the very eugenicist logics which were used to justify colonial oppression. This school of thought found feet in Britain in the early 1900s, along with concerns about falling birthrates and the poor health of young men: both issues which would affect the recruitment of soldiers to the army. 'Healthy' reproduction was central to the eugenicist vision, and some suffragists latched onto these ideas to emphasise the value and importance of women in British social life, and to push for the right to vote.[16] Eugenics was supported across the political and class spectrum, including by socialist women such as Beatrice Webb (who coined the term 'collective bargaining'), and Marie Stopes, the founder of the first contraception clinics, who saw birth control as a way to prevent the reproduction of people she deemed to be unfit parents. Eugenicist arguments in this era for effectively breeding better soldiers dovetailed with the creation of state-provided free school meals, and the 1911 National Insurance Act which provided a small sum of money towards the cost of childbirth. These legislative shifts, underpinned by anxiety around Britain's military deficiencies, in part paved the way for the creation of the welfare state, which would also be hailed as a feminist victory.[17]

Eugenics also placed sex workers in its crosshairs, framing them as 'vectors' of sexually transmitted infections (STIs), which were said to pose a threat to public morality, health and fertility. These particular arguments were later adopted by suffragists, including Christabel Pankhurst, who in her 1913 pamphlet *The Great Scourge and How to End It* advocated for an end to the demand for sex work, which was blamed for the spread of STIs ('race suicide!') in the name of preserving (non-sex-working) women's health and reproductive capacities. In the pamphlet, Christabel attributes the proliferation of STIs to 'immoral sexual intercourse', claiming that 'prostitution is the greatest of all dangers to the health of men,' and positing that the vote will 'empower' women to leave sex work.[18] Here, the interests of the suffragists and the police were closely aligned: the Home Office's data show that between 1900 and 1914, around 3,500 sex workers were arrested each year for soliciting.[19] The basis for harassment and arrests by police was directly linked to eugenicist ideas of desirable and undesirable characteristics. Particular targets included women who were in public spaces late at night unchaperoned, and those who were drunk or 'disorderly' – all key indicators of 'immorality' and 'weakness' within a eugenicist framework.[20]

Eugenics also provided the pseudoscientific basis for the expansion of the empire, which became a nucleus of women's organising in this era. Studies of 'imperial feminism' in the early twentieth century reveal how groups such as the Victoria League, which was founded by upper-class wives of colonialists connected to South Africa, and the League of the Empire, which was also set up by women, operated as propaganda machines for the colonial projects,[21] with a particular focus on strengthening bonds with the 'white dominions'. Some women imperialists held the view that a strong empire was reliant upon a healthy and productive working class back in the hub of the empire. They consequently threw their energies into issues of social reform, couched in the type of language the suffragettes would utilise a decade or so later; indeed the Victoria League's 'industrial committee' included figures such as socialist feminist Maud Pember Reeves, who would later become a suffragette, and its secretary was another suffragist, Meriel Talbot.[22] The question of building connections with people in Global South countries colonised by Britain, however, threw a spanner in the works of these imperial feminists, who discovered that their matronly sisterhood could not extend to racialised men, who, in their words, posed an inherent sexual 'danger'.[23] Imperial feminists upheld the idea of a hierarchy in which colonial subjects were infantile and inferior; eugenics provided the logic for adherence to this hierarchy.

At the turn of the century, women in Britain who were busy waxing lyrical about the empire were also beginning to raise collective concerns around voting rights. The National Union of Women's Suffrage Societies (NUWSS) was formed in 1897, when a number of women's suffrage groups merged under the leadership of Millicent Fawcett (also a founding member of the Victoria League). Fawcett's sister Elizabeth Garrett, the first woman to qualify as a surgeon and doctor in Britain, and Emily Davison, a teacher, had brought a petition to Parliament three decades prior with the backing of two MPs: Millicent's husband Henry Fawcett and John Stuart Mill. The petition was signed by women from different class positions and industries, including dressmakers, shopkeepers and blacksmiths' wives,[24] and was also notably signed by Sarah Parker Remond, a free Black woman, lecturer and abolitionist who was visiting Britain at the time. A key milestone of mainstream liberal feminist alliance with the state can be tracked back to these first-wave feminist demands: acceptance and integration *into* the state for an elite group, through the ability to vote for leaders and governments, achieved by a commitment to maintaining strict social hierarchies.

The petition's demands – the extension of the right to vote to include (some) women – was ultimately rejected. However, it sparked the formation of a series of smaller women's suffrage campaigns which later joined together as the NUWSS, and became known as 'suffragists'. The NUWSS's tactics have largely been historicised as 'peaceful', as they sought to make changes by playing within the rules of the existing system: by lodging petitions and seeking to expand the freedoms of middle-class and aristocratic women. Many working-class women were active in the NUWSS, but as the agenda set by the wealthy women in suffragist leadership roles failed to meaningfully encompass working-class demands, many splintered off into separate groups. The Women's Co-operative Guild, for example, was set up in 1883 to champion the interests of working-class women, and supported the suffrage movement. The Women's Co-operative Guild would later take a pacifist stance during the First World War and opposed conscription for fathers, and also campaigned for access to contraception and maternity rights.[25]

Some of these splinter groups focused particularly on worker's rights, such as the Lancashire and Cheshire Women's Textile and Other Workers Representation Committee, which was founded with assistance from Eva Gore-Booth (the daughter of a baronet) and Esther Roper, two former NUWSS members. Despite attempts by historians to heterowash their relationship, Roper and Gore-Booth were lifelong companions, likely in a queer partnership, and were buried in the same grave, which bears a quote from the ancient Greek poet Sappho on its head-stone: 'Life that is Love is God.' Roper and Gore-Booth would later write to Millicent Fawcett in 1906 about direct action tactics being utilised across the suffrage movement, which they thought alienated working-class women. They expressed concern that suffragists were likely to be stereotyped as embodying 'not only the opinions but the rough and ready methods and violent conduct natural to working women'. They suggested that working-class women were disinterested in 'futile police scuf-fles', as they faced more brutal police reprisals in comparison to their upper-class comrades.[26] Another suffragette, Lady Con-stance Lytton, famously proved this latter point. After receiving relatively gentle treatment due to her social status when she was imprisoned for a month for stone throwing, the next time she was arrested she gave a false name, and faced multiple force-feedings and physical assaults from prison staff.

Other women, however, felt limited by the 'constitutional' tactics adopted by the conservative NUWSS, and sought a more militant approach to try and secure wider gains. In 1903 another coalition of suffrage groups was formed in Manchester by Emmeline Pankhurst and her daughters Christabel and Sylvia: the Women's Social and Political Union (WSPU). The WSPU became known as the 'suffragettes': the diminutive '-ette' was used by the *Daily Mail* to try and belittle their efforts, but was quickly reclaimed. The WSPU's direct action tactics included chaining themselves to railings, smashing windows (on one activist's hammer was written 'better broken windows than broken promises'), damaging infrastructure by setting postboxes on fire, destroying telegraph cables and carrying out arson and bomb attacks on buildings including the Royal Observatory in Edinburgh and Holloway Prison.[27]

Unlike its leadership, the WSPU's membership was largely formed of working-class women. The group extended a certain degree of symbolic solidarity to women struggling for better working conditions, including to women coalpit workers in Wigan who faced attempts by the Miner's Union to push them out of the workforce,[28] and were visited by Annie Kenney, a uniquely prominent working-class figure in the WSPU. Sylvia Pankhurst also travelled around England and Scotland in 1907, meeting with working women, including in the West Midlands, where she spoke with and painted portraits of Cradley Heath chain and nail makers striking for a minimum wage, and in Glasgow, where she visited a cotton mill and almost fainted due to the poor ventilation that workers were subjected to.[29]

While the WSPU had a notably more working-class membership than the NUWSS, as historian Dr Sumita Mukherjee notes, the almost entirely white organisation didn't represent the demographic make-up of Britain in the early 1900s, which was 'very racially and ethnically diverse'.[30] A few suffragettes who were women of colour have received recognition for their involvement in early twentieth-century feminist movements in the UK, including Dr Susila Anita Bonnerjee, who organised with the Church League for Women's Suffrage, and Princess Sophia Duleep Singh, who organised with the WSPU and was arrested on multiple occasions.[31] Sophia was politicised to begin working on issues of social inequality after visiting India and observing the poverty and famine that Indian people faced at the hands of colonial administrators. Somewhat protected by her royal status, Sophia sold the suffragette paper in the grounds of Hampton Court Palace, where she lived. As academic Elizabeth Baker writes, in a sense this act was challenging the 'myths of British liberalism at the very site of their mythification'.[32]

Cracks in the movement

A decade after its formation, the WSPU faced a seismic political fracture. This split is not unique to the suffrage movement – fragmentation is perhaps the defining characteristic of British feminism, a detail that has largely been pushed into the background of historical accounts until relatively recently. While the more radical East London branch of the WSPU led by Sylvia Pankhurst was steered by the needs and interests of working-class women, the rest of the WSPU was increasingly guided by Emmeline and Christabel's more authoritarian and liberal agenda. Some suffragettes, disenchanted by the lack of working-class solidarity expressed by the elder Pankhursts, left the WSPU, such as the secretary of the WSPU's first London branch, Eliza Adelaide Knight, who used walking sticks. Knight was active in the WSPU's window-smashing campaign along-side her comrade Rosa May Billinghurst, who was a wheelchair user, and would use her wheelchair to ram crowds during actions. On her departure from the WSPU,[33] Knight remarked that the Pankhurst leadership had 'broken their promises to working women' by neglecting to work in solidarity with the labour movement.[34] Foreshadowing the First World War, which beckoned and would cleave further chasms in the movement, Christabel made it clear that there was no room for dissenting voices in the WSPU, stating, 'We want all our women to take their instructions and walk in step like an army!'[35]

In 1908, Emmeline Pankhurst stood trial at Bow Street Magistrates Court, accused of inciting the public to riot. Speaking from the dock she proclaimed, 'We are here not because we are law-breakers; we are here in our efforts to become lawmakers.' In the same speech, she lamented being denied the categorisation of 'political prisoner', noting that suffragettes would pass through the criminal-legal system without any kind of elevated status, and therefore 'shall be treated as pickpockets and drunkards'. Emmeline expressed her disdain for being lumped in with people who had been abandoned socially and economically – her feminism finding no common ground of solidarity with working-class people who experienced daily harassment from the state. The political position of the WSPU's leadership provides a cornerstone to our understandings of contemporary carceral feminism. By seeking solutions to feminist issues in the ivory towers of lawmakers and the judiciary, Emmeline and Christabel Pankhurst overlooked the lived realities of the majority of working-class women and their families, who were the primary punitive targets for law and order. As Emmeline's speech continued, she stated that she was seeking not a radical reconfiguration of society, but a seat at the table of decision makers and lawmakers; she wished for women to be granted 'that power, which every citizen should have, of deciding how the taxes she contributes to should be spent, and how the laws she has to obey should be made'.[36]

In contrast to the approach of her sister and mother, Sylvia Pankhurst had meanwhile aligned herself with the Labour Party and was dedicating her time to building a socialist women's movement which sought to ameliorate the poverty and inequality experienced by communities in London's East End. Both Emmeline and Christabel (who was at the time evading arrest while exiled in Paris), disapproved of Sylvia's work. In 1914 Sylvia was summoned to Paris, and she was told by Christabel that the Bow branch she led would have to sever ties with the WSPU with a 'clean cut'.[37] Reflecting on the meeting, Sylvia paraphrased her sister's admonishment: 'a working woman's movement was of no value; working women were the weakest portion of the sex; how could it be otherwise? Their lives were too hard, their education too meagre to equip them for the contest.'[38]

At Christabel's instruction, the Bow branch broke away from the WSPU and rebranded as the East London Federation of Suffragettes (ELFS). Other members also left the WSPU and formed new groups, such as the Women's Freedom League. The ELFS continued to agitate for demands levied by working-class women, and worked to improve the living conditions of families in the area. In dismissing the key issue of poverty and horrific working conditions endured by vast swathes of women in Britain, the elder Pankhursts failed in their feminist analysis to engage what would later be termed in feminist theory a 'materialist' approach. Materialist feminism encourages an understanding of the overwhelming and intertwined nature of patriarchal oppression within a system of capitalism which necessarily sorts humans into groups, and subsequently uses these categorisations to foster exploitation in order to accumulate wealth for a rich minority. Put simply by scholars Rosemary Hennessy and Chrys Ingraham in the late 1990s, 'class objectively links all women'.[39]

A materialist feminist analysis enables the letting go of an imagined generic 'woman' within feminist theory who by pure virtue of her gender is oppressed in the same way as all other women, instead foregrounding the material conditions of the lives of marginalised people as critical to our understanding of what liberation will involve, and how we might get there. Despite Emmeline Pankhurst's multiple imprisonments and violent treatment by police, the WSPU failed to examine critically the inherent violence of the criminal-legal system and the institution of the police, which continued to place working-class communities in particular in its crosshairs, and sought to maintain a landscape of poverty and deprivation.

Further fissures in the feminist movement were cracked open as the First World War dawned in 1914. The ELFS, led by Sylvia Pankhurst, maintained a pacifist stance, fighting to provide a safety net for families who had lost their primary wage earner, and campaigning voraciously for an end to the war. The ELFS opened a toy factory which employed local women, a cost-price restaurant (an initiative that the government would replicate in the Second World War), four health centres and a milk depot and progressive nursery.[40] A pub called the Gunmaker's Arms was taken over for this latter purpose, and renamed the Mother's Arms. Conversely, the NUWSS, led by Millicent Fawcett, expelled its pacifist members.[41] The WSPU also suspended their feminist agitating, and joined the war effort, including throwing their organising resources behind army recruitment drives, and handing out white feathers to men in civilian clothing, to humiliate them into enlisting.

The WSPU encouraged women to join the workforce in place of men fighting on the front, and were also involved in strike-breaking, on the basis that it was unpatriotic to stop working.[42] Christabel Pankhurst transposed the language of victimhood from women in Britain to the Allied powers as a whole,[43] with Germany (that 'male nation') now the perpetrator threatening the safety of the region. The *New York Tribune* reported that in a speech to Carnegie Hall Christabel made it clear that the suffragette's battles with the government did not detract from their patriotism, and that there was a clear connection between the police forces who had previously been their adversaries and the armies defending their safety. Christabel remarked, 'The allied nations are the nucleus of [a federated] world, and the allied armies the nucleus of the international police force.'[44] In August 1914 the government called a hiatus on the prosecution of suffragettes, and the Pankhurst leadership quietly accepted a grant from the government to organise a pro-war demonstration.

From police adversaries to women on the beat

The connection between suffragette activity and the police as a supposed force for good soon reached a potent nexus. Despite the reality of the police's violent attempts to suppress protes-tors – as documented in the wealth of photographs from this era that show officers physically assaulting women, beating them to the ground, and using their size and strength to overpower women – in 1914 two organisations began focusing on the issue of women police officers. The National Union of Women's Workers, known as the NUWW (which largely comprised non-working-class women) had plans for volunteer patrols made up of women, who would largely focus on preserving women's 'morality'. At the same time, the newly formed Women's Police Volunteers sought women's integration into the mainstream police force. Most notable is the political credentials of the co-founders and first women police officers in the Women's Police Volunteers. They included former suffragette Nina Boyle, who was political secretary of the Women's Freedom League; another suffragette and WSPU member, Mary Sophia Allen; and campaigner for animal rights and against 'white slavery' Margaret Damer Dawson.

For Allen, who had been arrested three times and force-fed in Holloway Prison, demands for women to be permitted into the police force emerged in response to the suffragettes' experiences of maltreatment by the police. In her 1925 memoir she reflected on 'how very unpleasant it [was] for an alleged woman culprit to be handled by men',[45] suggesting that the preferred solution to the violent reprisals experienced by suffragette protestors would have been to have women officers perpetrating the violence instead. Here we see the early leverage of 'feminist' arguments for 'diversifying' the police force. Boyle's motivation in this project was based on her concern that the criminal-legal system was failing women: the Women's Freedom League's newspaper *The Vote* had a regular column which both drew attention to the legal system's poor handling of GBV cases, and criticised the much more rigorous convictions of sex workers.[46]

Writing in *The Vote*, Boyle suggested that police work would be a good use of women's 'spare' time, stating, 'Appeals are being issued in every direction with a view to engaging and utilising for the benefit of the nation the vast reserve of feminine energy and ingenuity.'[47] Boyle reasoned that these activities could be best carried out by middle-class women – those with time on their hands. In 1915 the Women's Police Volunteers rebranded as the

Women's Police Service, at which point Nina Boyle broke away, dismayed at the militaristic route the organisation had pursued, which included enforcing a nightly curfew for women in a town in Lincolnshire where troops were stationed.[48] The Women's Police Service's early activities included harassing sex workers and surveilling working-class women employed at munitions factories in an attempt to diffuse unrest and prevent strikes.[49]

From suffrage to fascism

The desire to take part in the machinations of Westminster speaks to the persistent objective of some feminists to be further enmeshed in state-level decision-making. In a speech reportedly given in 1908 after her release from Holloway Prison, Christabel Pankhurst announced, 'The honour and safety of the country are in the hands of Parliament. Therefore, every patriotic and public-spirited woman wishes to take part in controlling the actions of our legislators.'[50]

The primary goal of mainstream feminism – that of inclusion within parliamentary democracy – after the First World War ended up producing a cohort of women who were politicised and primed to go toe-to-toe with the government in order to get a seat at the table, but without a political home as the activities of the WSPU and NUWSS died down. The entry of a number of prominent WSPU members into the police force itself, into right wing nationalism and later into fascism in the interwar period exposes the amorphous nature of feminist activity which is grounded only in an understanding of oppression rooted in gender inequality. Such feminisms fail to comprehend the context of racial capitalism – which complicates the primacy of misogyny as the most unifying facet of all women's experiences.

The 1918 Representation of the People Act enabled women aged over thirty to vote, if they lived in property that met a certain value threshold. This Act only enfranchised about 40 per cent of women in Britain and excluded the young and working-class women who, despite their actions often being relegated to the footnotes of history, had been at the forefront of the suffrage movement.[51] Having secured this much-sought parliamentary 'win', in the two decades that followed some former suffragettes made their transition into a politics of fascism. For these individuals, the strident, pro-military patriotism that suffragette groups such as the WSPU had demonstrated when war broke out in 1914 provided a seamless transition into the British fascist movement, spearheaded by groups such as the Imperial Fascist League and the British Union of Fascists (BUF) led by Oswald Mosley.[52]

Recruits to the BUF included Mary Allen (fresh from the Women's Police Volunteers), who threw herself into fascism in the late 1930s after meeting Hitler to discuss the police. Another suffragette who had been the WSPU's general secretary, Norah Elam, also joined the BUF, alongside suffragette Mary Richardson, who had previously slashed a Velázquez painting in the National Gallery in protest against the imprisonment of Emmeline Pankhurst. Richardson become the leader of the Women's Section of the BUF, and opined, 'I feel certain that women will play a large part in establishing Fascism in this country.'[53] In 1934 she also wrote an article in the BUF's periodical paper *The Blackshirt* explaining why she had embraced fascism. Richardson drew on her suffrage lineage as a spiritual training ground for her participation in the BUF: 'I was first attracted to the Blackshirts because I saw in them the courage, the action, the loyalty, the gift of service, and the ability to serve which I had known in the suffrage movement.'[54]

The shift from suffragette activities which involved brutal clashes with the state into a brand of politics which wholly embraced authoritarian rule and the police state itself is, of course, not the whole story of early twentieth-century British feminism. Many former suffragettes – who Elam decried as 'extinct volcanoes'[55] – did not become fascists, and in the decades that followed the legislative victory of 1918 moved onto different chapters in their lives. However, this trajectory from campaigning for enfranchisement to moving directly into right wing politics follows a clear logic: one of seeking acceptance by and integration into the state.

Richardson, Allen and Damer Dawson today might have identified as gay, however they did not have such language to describe themselves at the time.[56] This was true of many of the suffragists-turned-cops. Asa Seresin offers a compelling analysis of why this might be: the institution of the police offered a space where people gendered as women could, for example, explore more 'masculine' modes of dress, but without queering or destabilising the patriarchal status quo that requires the gender binary. The opportunity to wear short hairstyles and police uniforms operated in tandem with embodying the machismo and militaristic ideals of the force. These first women police officers sought to uphold oppressive and rigid patriarchal class structures through their police work, adopting what Seresin describes as a 'militant prudishness' and pursuing campaigns against what they understood to be symbolic assaults on womanhood as a category – such as sex work.

Feminist resistance to British colonial policing

The interwar period was a time of readjustment after four years of social destabilisation; definitions of British femininity had been disrupted as women had been required to act outside the domestic sphere while men were fighting on the front.[57] Schisms had also formed across the feminist movement, between pacifist and pro-military feminists. The extensive interwar feminist pamphlet collection of the London School of Economics (LSE) shows that focal issues for the remaining fragments of the feminist movement in the interwar period included the maintenance of international peace, women's role in the workforce and raising awareness of trafficking or 'white slavery'. Meanwhile, women in Britain's colonies in the 1920s and 1930s were joining movements against the gendered nature of British colonial oppression itself. These struggles placed dissidents in the colonies in direct confrontation with the police.

For women in the colonies, the use of collective working-class power was tantamount, as was the development of a variety of tactics other than making constitutional demands, and the linkage of fights for social and economic justice with the rejection of Britain's colonial domination. Protests in many cases concluded in clashes with police forces, who were tasked with quashing unrest and protecting the 'property' of the empire. The colonies were in effect 'laboratories' where forms of policing were tried, tested and refined before being brought back to target working-class people in the hub of the empire. Poet and theorist Aimé Césaire would later write that Nazism, for example, surfaced not through a random aberration in the German psyche, but through Hitler's borrowing of colonial practices of terror and control from other European powers: a colonial 'boomerang' of tactics.[58]

As academic Simin Fadaee suggests in their theory of social movements in the Global South, resistance in a context of colonial oppression is less likely to involve petitioning a government that doesn't recognise your humanity as equal to theirs.[59] Instead, protest takes the form of civil disobedience and everyday sub-version that disrupts the productive machinations of colonial administrations and businesses. For example, in South Africa in the 1920s, women protested against colonial laws that forced them to repeatedly pay for lodging permits and work passes to prove that their employment was 'legal'. Women pushed back against the laws and refused to buy passes, in some cases marching in their hundreds and tearing up their passes in front of the town's mayor.[60] Through these actions the women became politicised, joining trade unions and communist organisations which strengthened their resolve to resist; they would later enact a general strike in protest against pass laws. When colonial authorities attempted to take over the women-led beer-brewing industry in South Africa by restricting the sale to government municipal canteens and raiding women's houses, the women beer producers – backed by trade unions – retaliated by raiding the canteens.[61]

In the late 1920s women in India also participated in civil disobedience as part of the anti-colonial Quit India movement, breaking laws around the production and sale of salt, and boy-cotting British textiles and government-owned alcohol shops by blocking lorries and picketing businesses. This caused a huge drop in the colonial government's income, given that a quarter of government wealth came from alcohol sales.[62] The protestors were met with police violence and arrests. Imprisonment was so frequent that organisers would prepare each other for the likelihood of being locked up, with one organiser reassuring her comrades, 'Jails are holy places as Lord Krishna was also born in jail.' She continued, 'Such an argument was put forward while appealing to women citizens to come out of purdah (confine-ment) and get ready for the jails.'[63] Over 17,000 women were convicted in 1930,[64] and many women were imprisoned for up to a year for leading marches, giving speeches and holding meetings.

In the eastern Nigerian Aba Women's War in 1929, dance was used as a tactic of protest. These protests emerged in response to British colonial governance structures which had pushed women out of decision making, and sought to impose direct taxation on women as an extension of taxes that had already been levied against men in the region. The colonial system of appointing men as 'warrant chiefs' sought to replicate British patriarchal governance structures, and disrupted the previously collaborative forms of governance between men and women, shutting women out of political life. Thousands of women responded with a wave of protests, which included 'sitting on' the warrant chiefs by following them around, sometimes while singing and dancing through the night, in order to disturb their daily business and cause frustration.[65] The protestors also blocked roads, and targeted the symbols of British control, attacking banks and breaking into prisons to release prisoners.

Colonial police responded with force, shooting and killing over fifty women, and injuring many more. The taxation plans were ultimately scrapped, and the power of warrant chiefs was restricted, but in the period that followed the colonial police utilised the 1909 Collective Punishment Ordinance to put down any further unrest.[66] The ordinance was a piece of colonial law which gave magistrates powers to fine communities both for the lawbreaking of individual members, and for any refusals to co-operate or provide information in relation to lawbreaking.[67] While collective punishment would later be prohibited under international law, the British legal system continues to use a version of collective punishment under 'joint enterprise' laws, which particularly target young Black boys to this day,[68] again demonstrating the exchange of policing tactics which traverse from the colonies back to the hub of the empire.

Around the time of the Aba Women's War, as Nnenna Ifeanyi-Ajufo writes for the *Republic*, women in Tanzania (then British-controlled Tanganyika, formerly a German colony) also engaged in dance protests against British colonial rule.[69] After the dissolution of the German empire at the Treaty of Versailles, the British government established a network of new administrative and governance systems in Tanzania, including the Tanganyika Police Force and Prisons Service in 1919.[70] In the late 1920s, Tanzanian women joined *beni ngoma* dance societies, whose performances provided a form of commentary on the British administration, as well as on the re-emergence of missionaries in the region, and the impacts of the Great Depression.[71] *Beni* dances were stylistically influenced by other coastal dance practices in East Africa and satirically adopted the costumes of colonial military parades, parodying their drills, obsessive sending and receiving of reports, drinking and cigar smoking.[72] The *beni ngoma* also operated as mutual aid networks, and had distinct organising spaces for women and young people.[73] Concern about the subversive power of these societies led to their being placed under direct supervision of the colonial administration, and missionaries were encouraged to organise competing dance societies which would diffuse the power of the *beni ngomas*, and distract participants with disputes and fights.[74]

In the interwar period, women were also involved in labour disputes across British colonies. The extraction of raw materials such as oil and minerals was a function of the empire, if not its key function, and workers were paid low wages and worked in incredibly unpleasant conditions in order that Britain could shore up its wealth in the metropole. In many colonised coun-tries, women played a key role in articulating resistance to the colonial pursuit of capital through their own exploitation, and were met with surveillance and physical violence from colonial police. For example, in the 1920s in British-controlled Zambia (then Northern Rhodesia – named after the mining magnate and Oxford University donor Cecil Rhodes), copper mines functioned as a result of huge land grabs by the British South African Company as part of the colonising project. Miner's wives were permitted to live on the compounds, as bosses saw their presence as a stabilising force for their workers; however, the wives of workers in copper mines were involved in struggles for better conditions through protests and boycotts, and influenced the workers' demands.

Living conditions on the compounds were poor, and workers received low wages, so the miners' wives would supplement their partner's wages through selling beer and sex work. In some cases, the women led their own protests. In 1927, women at the Bwana Mkubwa mine refused to sweep areas of the compound that they weren't living in, and were supported in the boycott by the miners. On other occasions they protested by taking off their clothes in public. Women played a crucial role in labour protests through sharing information under the guise of 'gos-siping', and also passing on strike details while participating in *mbeni* dance performances (as in Tanzania), which again raised the concern of the colonial authorities. Strikes and unrest were met with violence from the Rhodesian police, including shoot-ings and fatalities.

Police violence was similarly meted out in response to a wave of labour rebellions across the Caribbean in the 1930s, as workers raised collective issues of low wages, underemployment and racist treatment by their bosses. Women across the Caribbean began unionising, and took up prominent leadership roles. In Trinidad, Thelma Williams and Daisy Crick joined the Oilfield Worker's Trade Union (OWTU), with Crick becoming the president of her local branch.[75] Factory and laundry worker Elma Francois co-founded the Negro Welfare, Cultural and Social Association (NWCSA) in Trinidad, which was explicitly inclusive of women, opposed male dominance in households and participated in strikes and hunger marches.[76] As Adam Elliott-Cooper details in *Black Resistance to British Policing*, in 1938 Francois was charged with inciting rebellion after resistance to police arrests led to the deaths of two officers: she represented herself in court and was acquitted of the charges.[77] The 1930s labour rebellions were underpinned by revolutionary demands: the workers demanded social and economic justice, with liberation from British rule as a prerequisite for achieving these goals.[78]

As the Second World War loomed in the mid-1930s, pan-Africanist author George Padmore drew comparisons between the rise of imperial fascism and Britain's own activities in African countries and India, explaining that the fascism brewing in Europe was British colonialism 'coming home to roost'.[79] Speaking at a rally held by a pan-African organisation in 1937, and reflecting on the labour rebellions of the previous years, writer C. L. R. James remarked (according to a Special Branch officer in attendance) that Caribbean people 'now knew how to enforce their rights, and how to remain solid in the face of threats and persecution. They were no longer afraid of strike-breaking police, militia and marines.'[80]

Just a decade later, when the Windrush generation arrived in Britain, the strikes and unrest which emerged in the face of violent structural inequality would continue a trajectory of dissent, begun with resistance to British colonial policing on Caribbean and African soil. The development of Black British feminism would stand firmly on the shoulders of this radical tradition, which understood the police as a crucial device of state violence.

Gender binaries in post-war Britain

In the wake of the Second World War, there was a general agreement across the political spectrum on how the country was going to rebuild, often referred to as the 'post-war consensus'. One of the key pillars of this approach was the creation of a welfare state, which included the founding of the National Health Service (NHS) in 1948 – which would be staffed in part by Black women as a result of recruitment drives across the Caribbean. The socialist feminist writer Vera Brittain described the welfare state as 'a product of the women's revolution' in that it signified 'the change in social values which that revolution accomplished'.[81] At the same time, the division of gender roles underwent a degree of reassertion, as men returned from fighting on the front and re-entered the civilian workforce, and a growing generational divide provoked anxiety about the destabilisation of 'social values'. Relative to their parents, teenagers in the 1950s had access to better education and housing, as well as leisure time and in some cases capital, enabling a certain engagement with consumerism as the post-war economy began to boom. As Prime Minister Harold Macmillan claimed in a 1957 speech at a Conservative Party rally, 'most of our people have never had it so good'.[82] Parents in the 1950s, meanwhile, had experienced two world wars, and had endured conscription, air raids and managing households through rationing, which only ended in 1954.

A new 'youth culture' threatened to undermine the post-war consensus, and police were tasked with suppressing it accordingly. The era after the Second World War is sometimes referred to as the 'golden age' of policing; certainly it represents a period in which the police doubled down on their attempts to be a symbol of national identity, and tried to cement their legitimacy in the popular imagination. In this so-called golden age, the strategies of 'policing by consent' were put in place, and attempts were made to convey the idea that the police are effective, nonviolent, fair and trustworthy. Meanwhile, Caribbean youth and their parents who were encouraged by the government to come to Britain to fill labour shortages and help rebuild the country in the late 1940s faced racism in the education system and in renting accommodation,[83] as well as violence on the streets. Black communities also faced a 'colour bar': segregation and discrimination, in some cases union-backed: in the labour market, including informally in the police force itself;[84] in the housing market; and in recreational spaces, such as pubs and restaurants.

These exclusions were all largely upheld by the police, who claimed to be tackling rising crime – in fact they were fighting everyday activities that were newly criminalised, from young people's use of public spaces to the mere existence of Black people in hostels, pubs, workplaces and more. Resistance to this structural inequality was necessarily built on the burgeoning anti-colonial support networks that had emerged in the 1930s and 1940s, such as the West African Student's Union (WASU) and the Indian Worker's Association (IWA), which organised interpretation services, legal assistance, work and accommodation for people who had newly arrived. Some IWA factions also joined anti-racist organising in collaboration with African and Caribbean activists.[85] The WASU provided hostels and social spaces for Black students in London, and increasingly placed pressure on the government to cede independence to the African countries it had colonised. The London Afro-Women's Centre was also set up by pan-African activist Amy Ashwood Garvey, providing accommodation and a restaurant, as well as a head-quarters for a number of small businesses run by women.[86] These spaces of organising and community, among others, provided pockets of respite among the hostility and deprivation faced by marginalised communities in 1950s Britain.

By the end of the decade, the country was undergoing a series of rifts in its narrative fabric. This attempted redrawing of gender divisions in the 1950s was more symbolic than actual; the ongoing entrance of women into (some segments of) the labour market, albeit largely in part-time work, as well as into trade unions, problematised the binaried spheres of 'work' and 'home'. This led to material gains for some women – although women's wages were still roughly half of those earned by men.[87] The inability of the dominant British consciousness to grapple with the figure of the woman as worker illustrates a yawning gap between oppressive, raced and classed ideals of women shut into their drawing rooms – the fragile, decorative 'angel in the house'[88] – and the reality of British society that was reliant upon grinding, tough and tedious work for women with real-life consequences for workers seeking to assert their rights.

While the economy was experiencing an upturn, Britain's imperial portfolio was being severely undermined as mainland African countries gained independence and transitioned away from oppressive colonial rule over the course of a decade. Conservative prime minister Winston Churchill had resigned in 1955 due to ailing health, and former Foreign Secretary Anthony Eden was installed as his successor, turning his attention to foreign policy as decolonisation accelerated and Britain flailed around trying to find solid ground. Eden stepped down from office after lying to Parliament about his involvement in Israel's invasion of Egypt and attempted seizure of the Suez Canal, which supplied a significant amount of oil to Europe. The invasion was met with threats of economic sanctions from the US, and strong resistance on the ground from communists, trade unionists and women-led groups, including the Women's Popular Resistance Committee in Cairo, who were trained in how to defuse bombs and shoot weapons.[89] Eden was succeeded in 1957 by Harold Macmillan, who was given a clear brief to re-stabilise British politics.

Not long after Macmillan's appointment, and not far from the Gothic spires of Westminster, untrammelled racism fuelled by politicians and media alike boiled over into attacks on Black people and their homes in West London's Notting Hill. Riots in both Notting Hill and also Nottingham were allegedly sparked by racist assaults against Black men who were in proximity to white women.[90] These attacks were underpinned by a political and legislative direction of travel which would continue to be overtly hostile to people arriving in Britain from the Global South. The Commonwealth Immigrants Acts in 1962, 1965 and 1968 would restrict entry to people with employment permits only, and the Acts were sped through in order to block Asian communities leaving East Africa.

In the wake of the riots, Frances Ezzrecco set up the Coloured People's Progressive Association, which would become the Conference of Afro-Asian-Caribbean Organisations (CAACO), organised by communist activist and journalist Claudia Jones.[91] Claudia Jones was also editor of the first commercial Black newspaper in Britain – the *West Indian and Afro-Asian Gazette* – which was the sponsor of another of her ventures that made its debut in

1959: the Notting Hill Carnival. The first carnival was organised under the slogan 'A people's art is the genesis of their freedom'; the intention was to celebrate the collective voice of Caribbean people in Britain, in defiance of the unrelenting violence meted out to communities from Parliament to the pavements.

Black and Asian women were a crucial part of anti-racist and community organising in this decade, and a bygone era of white feminist petitions and strident speeches from the dock seemed all but dead. Yet these stories about the formation of precious spaces, gatherings, uprisings, celebrations, services and publications pushing back against state racism were for many decades relegated to the footnotes of history. From the vantage point of 1959, it would have been impossible to predict that it would be the 1960s and 1970s that became synonymous with generally accepted ideas of contemporary feminism, or, as it was named at the time, 'women's liberation'.

2

A Symphony of Order and Chaos

Since none spoke for us, we decided we had to speak for ourselves.
Member of Birmingham Black Sisters (founded 1982)

The terror of a coercive police force, a highly trained military and the multifarious arms of the 'welfare' state are familiar ground to us.
Valerie Amos and Pratibha Parmar

In a piece of black-and-white archival video footage from 1968, a television reporter asks a handful of women in Cornwall whether they would consider forgoing wearing a bra.[1] The segment is broadcast in response to reports that American feminists are 'burning their bras' as a critique of women's oppression, and most of the interviewees appear vaguely nonplussed by the reporter's increasingly harassing line of questioning. In one scene the camera operator zooms in on a woman's chest while she is quizzed on whether bra sales are set to decline, and in another a man in a suit describes the garment as a 'very useful device'. This type of vapid journalism sits at the more banal end of the way issues understood as crucial to women's liberation in the 1960s – such as the 'rising hemlines' popularised by Mary Quant's miniskirt – were identified and represented in popular discourse. The timeless obsession with what women were wearing (or not) illuminates a particular framing of feminism as nothing more than media-savvy acts of personal disobedience and consumer choice, divorced from any social or economic context or strategy. At the more 'serious' end of the spectrum, the invention of the contraceptive pill is hailed as a feminist milestone of this era. Yet much like designer clothing, and media segments framing feminist activity as curious and whimsical as opposed to threatening to the social fabric, the contraceptive pill would initially only be accessible to wealthy women.

Contrary to the preoccupations of newspaper headlines, feminist organising in the late 1960s was much more than a series of stunts. A wealth of feminist activity was conceived within the amorphous umbrella of the 'women's liberation movement' (WLM): a collection of groups and organisations who were working and organising around gender inequality, and who were developing feminist theory and praxis through newsletters, conferences and other forms of collaboration. Many of these groups in their nascent forms had splintered off from left wing political organising spaces due to frustration with being belittled and sidelined by the men who claimed to be their comrades. Through its conferences, the WLM developed a set of demands: initially these focused on equal pay, access to jobs and education, access to contraception and abortion on demand, and free round-the-clock nurseries. In the years that followed, demands emerged around legal and financial independence; the right to a self-defined sexuality and an end to discrimination against lesbians; and freedom from violence and 'laws, assumptions and institutions which perpetuate male dominance and aggression to women'.[2]

Crucially, and despite the way in which this era has been represented until very recently in academic research, popular culture, mainstream media and more, the activities and participants in the WLM did not represent the totality of social justice and feminist activity in this era. There are overlaps between the WLM and the wider women's movement, Black feminism, anti-racism and labour organising (academic George Stevenson writes that 'feminism and class politics were sites of enormous cross-fertilisation'[3]), but the WLM also in different ways diverged from, ignored and actively hindered Black feminist work. As peace activist and co-founder of the London-based Black Women for Wages for Housework Wilmette Brown wrote at the time, 'Conventional racism underlies a still more dangerous racism by white women, more dangerous because it is in the feminist movement, which claims to speak for all women and to offer a better plan for the future.'[4]

In the 1960s and 1970s, Black feminists in Britain developed an intimate understanding of the precise interrelation between state violence and gender-based violence as it was underpinned by racial capitalism. Carceral feminists of this same era were at the exact same time developing feminist analysis with no such insights. It should be noted that in the 1970s and '80s, 'Black' was frequently used as a collective political term to include all people who are racialised and subjected to racism, much like the phrase 'people of colour' has been used since the 2010s. The slippage from 'Black' as a political category in the 1970s to the more ethnographic 'BAME/BME' (standing for Black, Asian and minority ethnic) in the 1990s is representative of the co-option and dilution of anti-racist political organising into milquetoast state 'multiculturalism' and local authority structures: the neoliberal horizon that this chapter sails towards.

Back in Parliament, the Race Relations Act was passed in 1968, in theory widening anti-discrimination legislation to also cover housing, employment and public services. Notably, its provisions didn't apply to the duties of the police force, or to any activity related to 'safeguarding national security'.[5] The Act was motivated by, according to debates in Parliament at the time, a desire for a society that was 'healthy' and 'free from tension'.[6] These aspirations allude to the events of the prior decade: the whipping up of popular racism by the media and politicians alike – including Wolverhampton MP Enoch Powell's inflammatory and racist 'Rivers of Blood' speech – and relatedly, attacks on Black people and their homes in West London's Notting Hill, and in Nottingham in 1958.

The Act would transpire to be little more than lip service; in 1979 the high commissioner in Bangladesh sent an internal memo to the British Foreign Office that read, 'it would be difficult to maintain that "discrimination" does not exist between the treatment of people entering Britain from the old and new Commonwealth' and that it was 'just unfortunate that most of those trying to cheat their way into Britain are coloured'. The high commissioner goes on to note that such discrimination is necessary in order to avoid Britain being 'saddled with hundreds of thousands of additional immigrants'.[7] The high commissioner was trying to justify the discrimination enacted by the border regime in this memo, because it had recently become an issue of heated debate and public scrutiny. The targets of this discrimination were, in this instance, specifically Asian women travelling to Britain to join their fiancés. Sometimes before departure, but mostly upon arrival, some Asian women were being subjected to intrusive and humiliating 'vaginal examinations' by border agents. These examinations were carried out

under the guise of pseudo-medical 'virginity testing', which the
Foreign Office claimed was necessary in order to 'prove' that
women were unmarried and therefore eligible for entry without
the certificates that married women were required to obtain in
order to come to Britain.

The web of mythologies constructed by the agents of the
British border concerning the assumed untrustworthiness of
Asian women, and the entitlement of the border regime to violate
Asian women's bodies which were coded as submissive and yet
sexually deviant, had deep roots in colonial projections of race
and gender.[8] AWAZ (the first Asian women's collective in the
UK) picketed Heathrow Airport, where some of the testing
had taken place. An article in the feminist publication *Spare Rib*
notes that AWAZ called for 'a public inquiry into the workings
of the immigration service'.[9] AWAZ were later joined in a sit-in
by both OWAAD (the Organisation of Women of African
and Asian descent)[10] and Southall Black Sisters (SBS), a GBV
organisation for Asian and African and Caribbean women,
formed in the wake of the police murder of protestor Blair
Peach at a demonstration against the far-right neo-Nazi party
the National Front. Protests also gathered in cities across India,
including Delhi, Mumbai, Chennai and Kolkata, with demon-
strators pasting signs on the high commission building that read
'Racists apologise' and holding placards that declared 'We'll
fight you on our land'.[11]

The protests against Heathrow virginity testing encapsulated
a nexus of the issues that necessitated the formation of new
feminist organisations which had a living, breathing knowledge
of state and border violence. They also demonstrated the nature
of Black feminist organising in its nascent stages in Britain: a
feminism that was internationalist in its outlook and connected

to global movements, and that utilised the tactics of pickets and protests, connecting with other anti-racist women's groups in sustained relationships of solidarity.

The workers united

Black and South Asian women arriving in Britain in this era brought with them not only a critique of British patriarchal and imperial power as deployed throughout the empire, but also knowledge and experience of workplace organising within a context of colonial oppression. South Asian women workers participated in labour movements and in the Asian youth movements, which were influenced in their radicalism and militancy by the Black Power movement in the US.[12] While Black and Asian women faced structural inequality and a particular vulnerability to violence and exploitation due to their gender, they observed men of colour within their communities and working alongside them who also faced precarious work, low pay and poor working conditions. Many women active within Black feminist spaces also drew on radical socialist traditions, as a founding member of OWAAD, Stella Dadzie, remarks, 'My internationalism came from my being a socialist. For me it was all about "Workers of the world, unite!" So my anti-imperialism came out of that experience, and I grafted it onto my feminism.'[13]

Due to this grounding in worker's struggles, Black and Asian women could understand their oppression as being produced through structures of racial capitalism. Conversely, the women's liberation movement is often considered to have been distinct from labour movements and working-class struggles. While the WLM was undoubtedly driven by young, middle-class women who were uninspired by the domestic realm they had been relegated to through becoming wives and mothers,[14] it also sprang from a combination of working-class women-led strikes and struggles for fair pay and improved working conditions. More attention has been paid to the former demographic.

The supposed distinction between 'feminist struggle' and 'class struggle' has led to what academic George Stevenson has described as the 'concealment' of working-class women's presence in British feminist movements more broadly.[15] Working-class women were fundamental actors within both the WLM and Black feminist organising in particular; simultaneously, high-profile strikes and pickets were led by women in recognition of the gendered nature of the oppression they faced in the work-place. These political positions and activities were inextricably linked, and fed each other with tactics, resources and knowledge. For example, sewing machinists struck at Ford Dagenham in 1968 over pay inequality between men and women workers and secured a pay increase, sparking the formation of the National Joint Action Campaign Committee for Women's Equal Rights, which in 1969 organised a demonstration in Trafalgar Square. Both of these actions contributed to the passing of the Equal Pay Act of 1970.[16]

The Cleaners Action Group was also set up in the early 1970s to improve working conditions, unleashing a significant strike at the Ministry of Defence building which secured a pay rise for the cleaners.[17] A documentary made by the Berwick Street Collective – *Nightcleaners Part 1* – depicts a woman (possibly Cleaners' Action Group organiser May Hobbs) speaking into a microphone at a protest for the campaign:

> They say the Women's Liberation is made up of middle-class and professional women. This is not true! A good proportion is made

up now of the working-class women. And I say, and I say to all of you, get out and fight now. Show the men we're not the little things we once were and they think we still are.[18]

Black feminist groups which overwhelmingly comprised working women did not always feel aligned with the priorities of white feminists and the WLM when it came to issues of economics, as one organiser notes:

> Groups like Wages for Housework were making a lot of noise, too. These were hardly burning issues for us – in fact they seemed like middle-class preoccupations ... we were more interested in getting paid for the work we were doing outside the house as night cleaners and in campaigning for more childcare facilities for Black women workers.[19]

In 1974 a strike was called by mostly East African Asian women at the Imperial Typewriters plant in Leicester in response to poor working conditions, racism within the workplace and flatlining pay while output expectations increased.[20] Despite being abandoned by their own union – one union negotiator stated that the workers 'have no legitimate grievances and it's difficult to know what they want ... Some people must learn how things are done'[21] – the workers embarked upon five weeks of strikes. Many workers were sacked in the process, and the factory shut down the following year, but the collective forms of organising paved the way for more strikes led by women of colour in particular.

One such strike unfolded in 1974 at the Grunwick film-processing factory, where South Asian women workers, including the formidable Jayaben Desai, walked out in protest after the sacking of a colleague.[22] The workers reported oppressive conditions in the factory, including strict rules that meant that women had to perform compulsory overtime, and were subjected to humiliating regulations, such as being obliged to 'ask' to use the toilet.[23] Desai and her colleagues came out on strike and demanded better working conditions. All 137 of the striking workers were sacked. Unlike at the Imperial Typewriters strike, the wider trade union movement initially came out in support of the Grunwick workers, holding huge demonstrations outside the factory, and Desai and her comrades also went on hunger strike. The large pickets were met with repression and pitched battles instigated by the Special Patrol Group (SPG), a branch of the Metropolitan Police which had been set up in 1961 to tackle 'public disorder' and were effectively deployed as riot control units and used to suppress activity in 'high-crime' areas – often in areas where Black and Asian communities lived.[24] The Grunwick strikes were the first time the SPG had been sent into an industrial dispute, both as a show of physical force and with covert and undercover surveillance tactics.[25]

Trade unions gradually withdrew support from the Grunwick strikers. The sacked workers were never reinstated, although workers who still held their jobs experienced some improvements to pay and pensions.[26] The strikes at Grunwick and Imperial Typewriters, among others, revealed the potency of collective action, and began to disintegrate racist stereotypes that migrant women and South Asian women in particular were docile and malleable, and could be easily exploited for cheap labour. The strikes sent a message that injustices would be met with resistance. As the general secretary of the Indian Worker's Association (IWA) Great Britain, Jagmohan Joshi, would remark, 'Never let it be said that the first generation of black immigrants played the role of uncle Toms. Far from it. They took to the streets and struck blows against all oppression … We won't sit back, we will hit back.'[27]

In the late 1960s and the 1970s, striking workers on pickets and at demonstrations were faced with the violence of the police, who protected the mutually beneficial interests of the state and business: maintaining a cowed, suppressed and impoverished workforce.

Black feminist power rising

Speaking to *Novara Media* in 2017, Marai Larasi, former director of GBV organisation Imkaan, commented,

> In the late '70s there was a real triangulation between political theory, the delivery of women's services, and broader black feminist organising … These organisations recognised you can't deal with gendered violence if you're not dealing with race, class and immigration status as well as gender. That perspective was often missing in the early women's movement.[28]

Alongside AWAZ, OWAAD and SBS, Black feminist organisations that emerged in this era included Asha Projects, which continues to provide refuges to South Asian women in south London, and Saheli, a refuge for women of colour also still operating in Manchester. The ASRAA refuge project of the AWRC (Asian Women's Resource Centre) was also set up in the 1970s, Newham Asian Women's Collective (later London Black Women's Project) began in 1981 and continues to deliver services to survivors, Shakti Women's Aid would be set up in Edinburgh in 1986, and Sahara Women's Refuge in Leeds was also founded in this era (and decommissioned in 2011). Not all efforts to set up refuges were fruitful: an application to the local authority to set up a refuge for Chinese survivors of abuse was refused; applicants were told to gather more 'proof' of domestic abuse among Chinese communities, despite a common understanding that the needs of Chinese survivors were not being met.[29] The socialist feminist organisation Brixton Black Women's Group (BBWG) was also founded at this time by former British Black Panthers, including Olive Morris, Beverly Bryan and Liz Obi.

A range of self-help groups also began organising, including Black Women's Mutual Aid, co-founded by Elouise Edwards in Manchester;[30] the Liverpool Black Sisters; and the Marxist socialist group Birmingham Black Sisters, which campaigned against issues such as deportations and domestic violence, as well as working in solidarity with struggles for national liberation globally.[31] Similarly, the Manchester Black Women's Co-op (later Abasindi Co-operative, which acted as a makeshift hospital during the 1981 riots in Moss Side) focused on unemployment and anti-police defence campaigns, and the United Black Women's Action Group in Tottenham, co-founded by Martha Osamor, set up a supplementary school and campaigned against stop-and-search by police.[32] The Scottish Black Women's Group was set up in 1985 to fill an urgent need for a space for Black women to organise together; its members stated, 'There is no platform in Scotland at present that provides us with a base from which to express our point of view'.[33] BBWG co-founder Olive Morris was also involved in the squatting movement, occupying a building which would become the Sabarr Bookshop, and together with Liz Obi squatted a disused launderette for use as a women's centre, which went on to assist many people in the community facing homelessness.[34]

Black feminist groups who in many cases rooted their work in socialism and Marxism focused on improving the material conditions of Black people's lives, which were impacted by inequalities across housing, work, education and beyond. In particular, Caribbean children faced discrimination in the British school system, with many Black children being assessed as 'educationally sub-normal' (ESN) and sometimes were 'bussed' to separate ESN schools.[35] This practice was 'justified' by a local authority report written by headteacher Alfred Doulton, who claimed that Caribbean children had lower IQs, and would bring down the attainment statistics of mainstream schools. The formation of the Black Parents Movement (BPM) was fundamental in mitigating this practice, as well as pushing back against suspensions and expulsions (a battle still being fought today by groups such as No More Exclusions). The BPM also led defence campaigns against police maltreatment, and worked in solidarity with pro-democracy initiatives, radical groups and trade unions in the Caribbean and Africa.[36]

Black women's organising was also crucial to the formation of supplementary schools in church halls, houses and basements. The schools, some set up by the BPM, focused on literacy, numeracy and Black history, but were autonomous from the state curriculum and received no funding.[37] Vitally, they provided a counterbalance to the racism that many children experienced in state schools, providing, as Diane Reay and Heidi Safia Mirza write, 'a context in which whiteness is displaced as central and blackness is seen as normative'.[38] Many teachers who had travelled to Britain from the Caribbean found themselves shut out of the profession and channelled their skills into the supplementary schools; Mirza explains that these schools were 'spaces of hope and transcendence underpinned by invisible women's work'.[39]

Literature and learning have always been foundational pillars of anti-racist and decolonial movements; the sharing of books and articles acted as a bridge to international struggles but also helped conceive of the future world that organisers were marching towards. Looking back at the sense of shared intention that came from actively engaging with Black writing among OWAAD members, co-founder Stella Dadzie later reflected, 'When I go into [comrades] houses, our bookshelves are all the same.'[40] Alongside the flourishing of supplementary schools, Black bookshops and publishing houses also formed, including New Beacon Books, set up by John La Rose (which narrowly avoided closure in 2021 thanks to huge community support); Bogle-L'Ouverture Publications, set up by Jessica and Eric Huntley; and the *Race Today* collective, which published regular political magazines.

Black bookshops, publishers and other community spaces, including restaurants, were important sites for gathering and organising, offering 'Pan-African sites of resistance',[41] and often facing racist attacks. The Mangrove restaurant in Notting Hill was raided twelve times between January 1969 and July 1970, and a public march to protest this harassment was met with police violence. A group of activists, including leader of the British Black Panthers, the Marxist Altheia Jones-LeCointe and *Race Today* co-founder Darcus Howe, dubbed the 'Mangrove Nine', were put on trial accused of inciting a riot. The Mangrove Nine argued for an all-Black jury, and mounted a successful defence which led to the most serious charges being dropped. In an unprecedented move, the judge presiding over the landmark trial stated that the police had displayed evidence of 'racial bitterness'.[42]

Black groups and community spaces did not limit the focus of their work to their own projects, but recognised and nurtured links and connections with broader anti-racist campaigns. For example, British Black Panther Mala Sen and the *Race Today* collective organised campaigns for housing within Bangladeshi communities through setting up the Bengali Housing Action Group, and John La Rose and *Race Today* co-organised the Black People's Day of Action in response to police and public inaction after a fire at house in south London's New Cross that led to the death of fourteen people, which witnesses attributed to a firebomb.[43] Two weeks prior to the attack, MP Jill Knight had given a speech calling for 'noisy' parties held by the Caribbean community to be banned, and suggested that other residents should take direct action against them.[44] Knight in fact continued to complain about 'West Indian parties' in Parliament, even in the wake of the massacre.[45]

Due to the radical and revolutionary roots of their work, Black organisers weren't simply seeking a seat at the table of white institutions, but instead critiquing the very existence of these institutions, through setting up alternative social and cultural structures. A member of the BBWG, Melba Wilson, later described how her experience of Black feminism in Britain differed from her experience in America, noting, 'Even though I had done a lot of work in the States, it was in the narrowly defined strictures of Black politics and basically it was all aimed at getting a piece of the pie, the American pie.'[46] Black feminist organising was also intimately tied to struggles for freedom from oppression globally, taking influence from US activists such as Angela Davis, but in particular finding affinity with liberation movements in the Global South in countries such as Angola, Mozambique, Zimbabwe, South Africa, Guinea-Bissau and Algeria.[47]

Black feminism focused on addressing immediate material concerns and threats to life, and connecting these struggles with global fights for independence. Some organisers, in contrast, understood the mainstream feminist movement, dominated by white middle-class women, to be less committed to the priorities of Black and working-class women. While it would be oversimplistic to suggest that Black feminist organising and the WLM represented stark binaries in terms of class, the material origins of these segments of the movements had a significant impact on their respective focuses and tactics. Stella Dadzie notes that the mainstream movement 'did focus very much on the body, on relationships with men, and on the glass ceiling'.[48] A practice emerged within the WLM of getting together in 'consciousness-raising' (CR) groups to discuss personal experiences on topics such as family, childhood, friends, colleagues, lovers, trauma, fears, dreams and more.[49]

CR groups were designed as a strategy of collective politicisation, theory creation and movement building. However, some Black feminist groups considered CR to be a 'petty bourgeois' distraction in comparison to the urgent issues they were battling, and raised concerns that the lack of structural analysis led to individualism rather than action.[50] Although some Black-led CR groups did exist, such as the Hackney Black Women's Consciousness-Raising Group founded by Dr Jan McKenley, the proliferation of CR groups within the WLM that worked on the basis that 'most women were like ourselves – not different' – led to the generation of a notable segment of feminist theory and praxis built upon the perspectives of white middle-class women.[51]

Much organised fightback against state violence is, and historically has been, carried out by those who would not use the term 'feminism' and eschew such categorisations, in part due to the association of feminism with individualism, whiteness and a lack of class analysis or critique of the colonial state. In

The Heart of the Race: Black Women's Lives in Britain, arguably one of the foremost texts exploring Black women's activism in Britain in the post-war era, one interviewee notes,

> What's the point of taking on male violence if you haven't taken on state violence? Or rape, when you can see Black people's bodies and lands being raped everyday by the system? ... the women's movement has acquired the image of the people who are running it [women who have come from a cushioned, middle-class background][52]

To centre white, middle-class women's organising in historical narratives risks erasing the theory, activities, struggles and successes of Black women's resistance. This historiographical sleight of hand continues to present a feminism of whiteness as 'central' and 'overarching' and Black women's organising as 'marginal' or 'specialist'. For example, one otherwise robust history of the 1970s British feminist movement recognises that OWAAD had a newsletter (*FOWAAD!*), but notes that 'the better known magazines were those that promoted the views of the movement in a *wide ranging way*'.[53] The confinement of Black communities' struggles to the footnotes of history facilitates feminist allegiance with the police.

Feminisms, the family and the essentialised body

The focus on 'the body', as Dadzie notes, included the topic of reproductive health, and in particular the issue of contraception and abortion. Black women experienced consistent racism in healthcare settings, and often felt that professionals sought to limit and control the size of their families. In contrast, white feminists in the 1960s had been campaigning for increased access to abortion and contraception, leading up to the 1967 Abortion Act and the contraceptive pill being made available to unmarried women in the same year. This victory has its own sinister back story: as historian Paula Akpan notes, the contraceptive pill was tested on women without their informed consent, including in the notorious Río Piedras trials in Puerto Rico.[54] The Pill was approved for use despite having serious side effects, many of which in Río Piedras were dismissed as psychosomatic.[55] Feminists in the US lobbied senators to raise the issue of side effects – in 1967 the Pill had three to seven times the oestrogen levels of today's Pill[56] – which led to the first mandated health warnings on medicines, and forced the dose of oestrogen in the Pill to be lowered.

Back in the WLM, feminists recognised the barriers many women faced to accessing safe and supportive medical treatment, and set up independent pregnancy testing and post-result counselling. As has been documented by historian Jesse Olszynko-Gryn, although these services were often set up to assist women who didn't want to be pregnant, organisers came to realise that many women seeking tests did want to be pregnant, including those who were experiencing fertility issues. This led to an often-overlooked expansion of feminist praxis, which in some cases recognised that reproductive justice was not limited to preventing pregnancies.[57]

The experiences of Black women in healthcare were distinctly different to those of middle-class and white women; for example, a dubious contraceptive injection called Depo-Provera was administered to Black women in the UK and the US (despite being banned) and also across the Global South, including in India and Zimbabwe, sparking a campaign in Britain led by Black feminist groups including AWAZ and OWAAD. At their 1979 conference, OWAAD members noted that Depo-Provera was being given to Black women despite known side effects such as cancer, bleeding and permanent sterility, as Black women were euphemistically considered a 'contraceptive risk'.[58] The differential treatment that Black women faced in healthcare settings became a point of tension within the feminist movement. Where Black women did seek abortions, some were asked to provide proof of immigration status before advice or treatment, and faced additional hurdles which were not centred in the mainstream movement's campaigns on this issue.

As Professor Judith A.M. Scully notes, Black feminists did not relate to the 'reproductive choice' framework which was concerned with women's right to choose from a range of reproductive health products or services, and were particularly aware that the 'choices' available to them were often dangerous and without their consent, and in some cases led to temporary sterilisation.[59] Many Black feminists felt that contraception and abortion were being encouraged for Black women as a method of repressing Black families and limiting the Black population; this understanding was rooted in the fact of colonial and eugenicist logics underpinning the evolution of contraception as a field. As one Black organiser noted,

> We didn't want to become part of the white women's movement. We felt they had different priorities to us. At that time, for example, abortion was the number one issue … they seemed like middle-class preoccupations. To begin with, abortion wasn't something we had any problems getting as Black women – it was the very reverse for us![60]

While feminist movements broadly grappled with the topic of 'the family' through discussion in CR groups and the emergence of the first domestic violence refuges which we explore in this chapter, Black and working-class women's ability to simply divest from men and nuclear family structures was problematised by their lived realities of structural inequality. As Surinder Guru, Shirin Housee and Kalpana Joshi write in their powerful chronicling of the work of the Birmingham Black Sisters, 'The family, therefore, protected Black people from racist hostilities just as it provided a haven for working class families away from capitalist exploitation.'[61] The mainstream feminist movement's atomising of gender-based violence as being perpetrated by individual men, for which the solution was social abandonment of those individuals, provides a cornerstone to carceral feminist logics and punitive approaches which continue to alienate survivors seeking support from GBV organisations to this day.

Another key focus for the WLM was on anatomy, in particular genitalia and reproductive organs. Feminists seeking in particular to counter the discrimination and violence of healthcare and gynaecology conducted 'self-examination' of their cervixes, utilising speculums, torches and hand mirrors to demystify and connect with their own bodies, reclaiming self-knowledge outside the gaze of medical professionals.[62] Dr Jan McKenley, who performed a self-examination of her cervix at a women's health retreat in the 1970s reflects, that the practice 'probably epitomises the best of women's liberation for me because I looked at my vagina and it was beautiful, and feminism gave me my body'.[63] The practice of self-examination was advocated in a short pamphlet, *Our Bodies, Ourselves*, published in 1971 by a collective of women in the US. The collective gently encouraged readers to 'take a mirror and examine yourself. Touch yourself, smell yourself, even taste your own secretions. After all, you are your body and you are not obscene.'[64]

As with CR groups, some Black feminists saw the practice as indulgent and a distraction from more urgent issues. The preoccupation with reproductive organs being a unifying dimension to women's experiences was central to a school of thought and activity within the broader WLM termed 'radical feminism'. Radical feminism sought to dissolve the biological determinism that created fixed and oppressive roles and expectations for women on the basis of their gender. However, radical feminism's rejection of biological determinism and desire to 'eradicate gender' through pushing to coalesce around a singular, collective experience of gender and oppression in many cases elided into definitions of the category of 'woman' expressed in limited, anatomical and binary terms.[65] Biologically essentialist radical feminist thought has also engendered an assumed shared battle against 'male' violence and its presumed handmaidens, such as pornography, sadomasochism (S&M) and sex work.[66] These ideas were outlined in foundational radical feminist texts such as the 1969 Redstockings Manifesto, which also centres the perspectives of white, middle-class, university-educated women and sweeps aside any suggestion that oppression on the basis of gender is experienced differently according to racialisation, class and more:

> We identify the agents of our oppression as men. Male supremacy is the oldest, most basic form of domination. All other forms of exploitation and oppression (racism, capitalism, imperialism, etc.) are extensions of male supremacy ... We repudiate all economic, racial, educational or status privileges that divide us from *other* women.[67]

The framing of 'male violence' as the target of radical feminism reinforces the idea of fixed roles of 'victim' and 'perpetrator', which leads directly into carceral solutions to violence, the mentality being that if the perpetrators can be isolated, rounded up and thrown in prison, the world will be safer for women as a generic category. I spoke about this logic with Koshka Duff, who explained that the emphasis on male violence within carceral feminism is reliant on 'the idea of an inherently morally superior sort of womanhood', and on the resultant suggestion that placing women in charge of existing political institutions would be a wholesale improvement – despite firm evidence, as we will explore, of women using political power to endorse and reinforce oppression. Duff explains that there is a 'short step' between this attitude and the patriarchal, Victorian view of white women as the pathologically kind and gentle 'domestic angel'.

In 1970, Germaine Greer published her bestselling book *The Female Eunuch*, pitched as a revolutionary call to arms for women to free themselves of sexual repression and the confines of marriage, which – harking back to John Stuart Mill – she refers to as 'the crudest form of colonization'.[68] The transphobia of *The Female Eunuch*, mostly implied in its original edition, is graphically rendered in a twenty-first anniversary edition of the book, in which Greer refers to transgender women as 'men who mutilate themselves and are given passports as statutory females'.[69] Greer also draws on religious essentialism in the updated edition, remarking that the repressed 'female eunuch' can be found 'triumphant even under the veil'. *The Female Eunuch* also makes a passing, but revealing, suggestion that men in prison are chromosomally inclined towards criminality. These key themes – that of both gender and religious essentialism, and the related belief in a cellular-level criminality of men who commit violent acts – become foundational pieces of carceral logic, as we shall see.

From and towards multiple feminisms

The focus on 'man the oppressor' and 'the body' were just some of the issues that alienated some Black feminists from the wider WLM. In some other areas, solidarity was effectively formed across white- and Black-led groups, as BBWG member Gail Lewis reflects:

> There was, for example, a very active South London Women's Charter group that was a predominantly white women's organisation but very much focused around questions of working class women's relationship to work/employment. Some of the early Brixton Black Women's Group (BWG) women felt that was a women's organisation that they could have at least some sympathy with because it seemed to be related to questions of class.[70]

However, many Black feminists felt like they were begrudgingly 'given' space at the feminist table, as Amrit Wilson reflected on her time working on *Spare Rib*:

> You *always* felt excluded, you *always* felt like an outsider who was somehow being given space ... there was always the issue of 'what can we do for you,' right, 'you poor, poor things, what can we do for you?' ... often I was particularly notorious as somebody horribly aggressive because so many women *cried* when I spoke.[71]

Wilson notes that she did keep writing at *Spare Rib* and it gradually improved its approach; a success in itself. Elsewhere, however, some feminist white women made symbolic gestures of anti-racism, while failing to recognise the racism embedded in their day-to-day organising. Such dynamics were present in one of the first Reclaim the Night marches (which are still organised today) which was held in Leeds in 1977. The march was organised by feminists in response to police inaction after a spate of murders, predominantly of sex workers, carried out by Peter Sutcliffe, who would be dubbed the 'Yorkshire Ripper'. The police had been unequivocal in their disdain for sex workers, at a press conference stating that Sutcliffe 'has made it clear that he hates prostitutes. Many people do. We, as a police force, will continue to arrest prostitutes. But the Ripper is now killing innocent girls.'[72] The attorney general commented, 'Some [of the victims] were prostitutes, but perhaps the saddest part of the case is that some were not.'[73] The marches also represented a contestation of police advice that women should stay indoors at night in order to avoid being murdered. The suggestion of a 'curfew' for women is a recommendation that would be made throughout the decades that followed, in the wake of the murders of women.

The Leeds Reclaim the Night march sought to push back against the institutional sexism and classism of the police; however, the march alienated Black communities by travelling through primarily Black neighbourhoods and therefore increasing the risk of police contact and harassment for people living in those areas.[74] The choice to march through Black neighbourhoods holding flaming torches, reminiscent of neo-Nazi marches by groups such as the Klu Klux Klan, was also incredibly alarming, as was the perceived association being made between acts of rape and Black men – again calling upon the centuries-old racist stereotype that Black men are inherently inclined towards sexual aggression and predation.[75] Similar concerns were raised in response to Reclaim the Night marches held in the East London borough of Hackney in 1982, and in Cambridge in 1984, which is particularly notable in that organisers called for 'better policing'.

At this time, Black feminist groups were actively organising against the 'sus' laws which gave the police powers to stop, search and arrest any person suspected of 'loitering with intent to commit an arrestable offence' under Section 4 of the 1824 Vagrancy Act. Sus laws effectively meant that the police could harass anyone they wanted, on the pure basis of a hunch or corroborated opinion of two police officers, meaning that these searches were incredibly difficult to challenge. Black feminist organisations collaborated with other groups such as the BPM and the Black People's Organisations Campaign against Sus (BPOCAS), and Black women such as Mavis Best organised to monitor, challenge and resist these policing tactics. While Section 4 was repealed in 1981 after a Home Affairs select committee received damning evidence from Best, BPOCAS and others, the swift introduction of the Police and Criminal Evidence Act (PACE) just three years later effectively brought sus laws back under the guise of 'stop and search', and Black and anti-racist campaigners continue to push back against these laws to the present day.[76]

Given this context, white feminists' continued reliance upon policing as a response to gender-based violence revealed a one-dimensionality to their theory and praxis of building liberatory futures. In her comprehensive study of white women and race in the WLM, academic Natalie Thomlinson suggests that the WLM did hold a *position* of anti-racism but failed to translate this position into action, noting that 'rather than being simply racist, one of the interesting contradictions within the WLM lay in the gap between the awareness of many white feminists of the issue surrounding race, and their inability to translate this awareness into action.'[77]

Thomlinson writes that white feminism in the 1970s was concerned with personal identity and what would develop into the discourse of 'lived experience' – a phenomenon that Thomlinson refers to as the 'autonomous struggle paradigm'. This expression of feminism was perhaps more comfortable with anti-fascism, within which critiques of gender inequality and toxic expressions of masculinity were a key feature. White feminism was less comfortable grappling with racism, however, which required a complication of the primacy and exceptionality of gender as a site of oppression. This was evident in, for example, the emergence of 'soul-searching' anti-racist consciousness-raising groups which laid heavy emphasis on anti-racist correctives of the self being a feminist end, rather than a route into working in solidarity with Black and anti-racist groups.[78] Beyond such activity, attempts to bring race onto the mainstream feminist agenda were often seen as a 'diversion', and as Marxist feminist scholar Hazel V. Carby wrote at the time, 'White women in the British WLM are extraordinarily reluctant to see themselves in the situation of being oppressors, as they feel that this will be at the expense of concentrating on being oppressed.'[79] Carby voices the consistent stumbling block of white feminism: the cartoonish representation of women as passive victims only, divorced from any structures of inequality other than gender, and incapable themselves of wielding or inadvertently benefiting from dynamics of power along lines of class and race.

In the 1980s Black women increasingly wrote about and documented their frustrations with the racism of WLM. White feminists' focal points for activism, such as the formation of the anti-nuclear women's peace camp on a Royal Air Force base at

Greenham Common in 1981, continued to overlook the pressing demands of Black feminists. Guru, Housee and Joshi note,

'They seemed oblivious to issues facing Black people ... That Third World societies were devastated by wars fought by non-nuclear weapons with guns and bombs were all ignored.'[80]

Black feminists, including Valerie Amos, Pratibha Parmar and Madhu Kishwar, query why English feminist movements in this era were not mobilising with the same vigour and ferocity against Britain's role in mining, expropriation of land and warmongering in Britain's 'own backyard': the north of Ireland.[81] They also point to the underlying white fragility in the idea of a 'peace camp', as the mere existence of Black activists, let alone occupation of a military base, has always been assumed to be an aggressive affront to 'keeping the peace'. As Kishwar reflected in 1984,

A movement for disarmament begins with a movement against the use of guns, the everyday weapons. Here (in Britain) you may have a fear of nuclear holocaust and death and destruction – in India millions die of water pollution – that is a more deadly weapon for women in India.[82]

Yet as the decade unfolded, Black and white feminists grappled with these differing priorities, and did increasingly attempt to work in coalition. As Amos and Parmar note,

The autonomous activities of Black women ... forced the white women's movement away from a celebration of universality and sameness, to be concerned with the implications of differences among women's experiences and understanding the political factors at work in those differences.[83]

Thomlinson's research suggests that collaboration (and cohesion in general) was possibly more successful among smaller, more long-standing feminist groups where organisers got to know each other well, and was less fruitful in larger cities where newer groups (including 'mixed' groups comprising white and Black members, largely founded by white women) clashed internally, and with each other on the feminist 'scene', and had a tendency to become entangled in theoretical and academic back and forths.[84]

Staking territory: order and chaos within the movement

Feminist groups in Britain in the 1970s and early 1980s comprised an ecology of informal, unfunded 'collectives'. In many cases, collective organising was explicitly aimed at, and articulated in accordance with, feminist principles, as well as revolutionary, socialist and communist political traditions.[85] OWAAD, for example, was formed as an umbrella organisation which brought many smaller groups together at their conferences and connected them via their newsletter. Black feminist organisations also made connections with other women's groups organising internationally and worked with them in solidarity against the sprawling web of colonial oppression. This commitment to collectivity in some cases would later shape-shift into the creation of more formally constituted organisations, while for others it would contribute to the demise of groups. Jo Freeman, who was involved in CR groups in Chicago in the 1970s, writes incisively about the tyranny of 'structurelessness' in feminist groups, and is worth citing here at length:

Contrary to what we would like to believe, there is no such thing as a structureless group. Any group of people of whatever nature that comes together for any length of time for any purpose will inevitably structure itself in some fashion. The structure may be flexible; it may vary over time; it may evenly or unevenly distribute tasks, power and resources over the members of the group. But it will be formed regardless of the abilities, personalities, or intentions of the people involved ... Thus structurelessness becomes a way of masking power, and within the women's movement is usually most strongly advocated by those who are the most powerful (whether they are conscious of their power or not). As long as the structure of the group is informal, the rules of how decisions are made are known only to a few and awareness of power is limited to those who know the rules. Those who do not know the rules and are not chosen for initiation must remain in confusion.[86]

In an oral history project hosted by the British Library, the first national co-ordinator of Welsh Women's Aid in the 1970s, Jane Hutt, similarly reflected on her experiences of navigating power dynamics: 'The hardest things in the women's movement, and that goes through all of the discussions we've had, has been the fact that women can oppress other women.'[87]

The masking of power within organisations led to the default prioritisation and deprioritisation of issues according to whether they were deemed 'central' or 'marginal' to those holding power (consciously or otherwise). Black lesbians, for example, found themselves caught between external and internal scrutiny. From the outside, they battled assumptions that Black families were particularly homophobic, a myth that one organiser explained misunderstands the more obvious fact that 'the security links we need with our families/communities are stronger,' and therefore the stakes of 'coming out' were much higher than for white, middle-class lesbians.[88] In an interview in feminist magazine *Trouble and Strife* in 1990, BBWG member Gail Lewis notes,

> In the late '70s/early '80s lesbianism was not seen as a political issue; it was seen as something you did privately and was therefore your own business. We really managed to hang ourselves up with that because like every other Black organisation at that time, we had a notion of the Black community as traditional, as homogenous and as unable to deal with difference.[89]

Meanwhile, within Black women's groups, some understood that sexuality was an important issue whereas others tried to push the topic off the agenda. Paula Akpan writes that the BBWG initially 'dithered' over whether to invite Black lesbians to gather in their space, this tentativeness attributable to 'the AIDS moral panic, an increasingly homophobic climate stoked by the media, and the steadfast belief that lesbianism was a bourgeois white import that had no place in Black communities'.[90] In the end, the BBWG did end up hosting a Black lesbians' group which was profoundly important to its members, who provided support and solidarity to each other. This caused some dissent among members who were concerned about whether hosting a lesbian group in their space would affect their status within the wider Black community.[91]

Similarly, within OWAAD, lesbian members had to 'keep it quiet'. As Salma Al-Hassan explains, there was a general sense that sexuality was not a 'pressing issue', that the more 'politically respectable' topic was that of gender relations.[92] Some OWAAD members were concerned that a focus on sexuality would detract from the group's wider analysis of the interplay of racism and classism in women's lives, and constitute a shift into 'identity-based' organising. However, in a *libcom* article in 2017, members noted that this approach in fact 'served as a guise NOT to discuss the construction of sexual orientation (rather than sexuality in its broadest sense) at all'.[93]

In spite of the backdrop of intense structural oppression and discrimination, lesbians who also experienced racialised forms of oppression did get together and begin organising in collectives. These groups included the Camden Black Lesbian Group in Camden, a Black Lesbian Group in Waltham Forest, and the Chinese Lesbian Group. In the mid-1980s the first national Black lesbian conference – Zami I – was held in London and attended by over 200 women. These gatherings all provided unique and vital spaces for lesbian women of colour to meet and support each other; in an interview with artist Meera Shakti Osborne, a member of the Chinese Lesbian Group reflected, 'I thought I was the only Chinese lesbian in the world at the time so this was like "wow! I've got this amazing gang of friends that look like me".'[94] Black lesbians were specifically subject to intensified structures of oppression due to racism and the colonial legacy of anti-gay laws which were implemented across the empire by Britain: they were fighting oppression on multiple, intersecting fronts. Black lesbians were also facing the struggles encountered by white lesbians in terms of state and public homophobia, as well as internalised homophobia, in combination with structural inequality along lines of class and race that sought to splinter relations between Black men and women (as well as among Black women), in ways that required a huge amount of work and energy to overcome.

Internal conflicts around sexuality were happening across the WLM and also among different lesbian organising groups within and adjacent to it, from lesbian collectives focused on research and information sharing such as the Minorities Research Group to the 'rebel dykes' of the London punk and anarchic lesbian scene of the 1980s, who differentiated themselves from second-wave feminists who were 'seemingly mainly interested in meetings and theories and political lesbianism, with its anti-sex rhetoric'.[95] Rebel dykes joined the Greenham Common peace camp, set up a lesbian S&M club and abseiled into Parliament to protest against Section 28. At times lesbian feminist organising overlapped and interlinked with that of the broader gay liberation movement; however, many lesbian groups organised on issues specific to their community, and some segments of the lesbian community actively severed connections with the gay movement due to their experiences of misogyny from gay men.[96]

Some lesbians loosely grouped under the banner of being 'revolutionary feminists', and advocated for separation from men and sometimes also heterosexual women. Meanwhile, some Black feminist lesbians understood the pursuit of separatism as a 'luxury', quite literally: a key pamphlet written by the Leeds Revolutionary Feminists entitled *Love Your Enemy? The Debate between Heterosexual Feminism and Political Lesbianism*, which proposed separatism, was composed in a holiday cottage in Yorkshire.[97] Some Black feminists also observed that revolutionary feminism had a tendency to engage imperial arguments, including refusing Asian men entry into the country, and suggesting that women in the north of Ireland should support the presence of British troops because the Republican movement was dominated by men.[98]

The WLM often operated 'women-only' spaces, and this idea was promulgated and expanded by radical feminist lesbians, some of whom also embraced and experimented with these modes of lesbian-only communal living. A related concept was that of 'political lesbianism', which rejected all romantic and sexual relationships with men as inherently violent, coercive and non-consenting in the context of patriarchy ('every woman who lives with or fucks a man helps to maintain the oppression of her sisters and hinders our struggle'[99]), and posed the choice to be lesbian as an inherently political act. Political lesbianism was and continues to be contentious – the rigid proposed 'dichotomy'of sexuality being related *either* to nurture and personal choice *or* to nature is a false separation, as queer people do not monolithically experience their sexuality, which is also rarely static within a lifetime. In addition, the gatekeeping of 'true feminism' as requiring the disavowal of men represented yet another limitation and judgement placed on the scant 'choices' available to Black and working-class women. While some Black lesbian organisers in the 1980s clearly articulated their sexuality as being political and liberationary, and for many a journey of discovery alongside and in step with their politicisation, they were also clear that lesbian separatism enforced a hierarchy of oppression, with 'sexual oppression being more devastating than others'.[100]

The final WLM conference in 1978 was marked by disputes over separatist revolutionary demands, among other disagreements on issues of race and class. This discord was not unique to the WLM, but was part of larger discussions around sexuality within feminist movements, a critical point of nuance which is often overridden by the desire to locate a singular 'reason' for the fragmentation of the WLM.[101] The Black feminist movement also experienced fractures when it struggled to embody a range of perspectives, in particular those of Asian women, and between those advocating for a more internationalist, as opposed to local, focus.[102] As Amina Mama wrote in 1995, 'Issues of identity were

continuously problematic terrain within a black women's movement committed to the ideal of unity, yet faced with the reality
of cultural and political diversity within its ranks.'[103]

OWAAD was originally set up as the Organisation of
Women of Africa and African Descent, but later expanded its
remit and its name to include Asian women; Al-Hassan notes
that this almost symbolic 'adding in' of Asian women from the
beginning perhaps points to a larger issue that would lead to
the group's fragmentation.[104] While solidarity was posed as a
goal, Mama makes it clear that asserting an 'objective reality'
of unity did not match up to the day-to-day experiences of
organising among 'disparate groups of women'. Similarly,
OWAAD members have reflected that the group came to an end
due to the 'differing positions on the relevance of feminism to
our struggle ... the organisation could no longer project itself
as a united front'.[105]

In some senses, this complex negotiation of priorities and
tactics within organising spaces was a repetition of history for
Black feminist organisers, who had set up separate organisations
due to men within the anti-racist movement not understanding the centrality of gendered oppression to their struggles.[106]
Women had been central in groups such as the British Black
Panthers, for example, but began to meet separately when they
grew frustrated with trying to organise 'in a situation where
we were constantly regarded as sexual prey'.[107] OWAAD co-
founder Stella Dadzie has commented that women were often
positioned in anti-racist and Black liberation movements as
'minute-takers, typists, and coffee-makers but hardly ever as
political and intellectual equals',[108] and so they decided to channel
their energies into Black feminist organising. This segmentation
led to accusations being levelled at Black women that they were

'splitting the movement' and draining organising power from groups that were already struggling to keep afloat.[109]

The need for organising around gendered oppression had also been a key locomotive for groups set up by and for Asian women, many of whom had experienced the Asian Youth movements as being dominated by men. Black and Asian women were aware that raising awareness of issues such as interpersonal violence would likely result in racist backlash depicting their communities as pathologically violent; this had led to self-censorship and silencing among survivors. The legacy of this continued into women's organising spaces: a member of Birmingham Black Sisters notes that the abusive actions of 'comrades' from the wider anti-racist movement were not discussed among their group. Organisations led by men would, in turn, describe feminist organisers as 'bourgeois' or, as in one issue of the Indian Worker's Association newsletter, tauntingly as 'western feminists'.[110] Black women organising around issues of structural inequality were constantly encountering pressure to compromise on their political positions – to decide whether they were women, or whether they were Black.

In the late 1970s women's liberation was ascendant. Black, working-class and materialist feminists understood intimately how the state perpetrated both everyday and extreme violence through the police, and via imperial interventions overseas. The state and its agents were clearly oppositional to the attainment of justice and liberation for marginalised communities. At the same time, white feminists who lacked analysis of power and inequality, and centred their energies around addressing 'male violence' only, failed to understand the ways in which, for example, men who were raced and classed were also oppressed. In the same way as Black women could not 'choose' between being subjected to structures of either sexism or racism, Black men could not only opt to benefit from the privilege of being a man, when their experiences *as* men were routed through racism and classism. As we explore in the next chapter, when Black feminists began 'formalising' their organising and constructing their own infrastructure, a golden era of funded and sustained work would bring bonds of obligation to the state and associated reliance on police and prisons, which would irrevocably change the shape of the feminist movement's ecology.

3

The 'Sectorification' of Radical Struggle

In order to legitimise itself, neoliberalism does need carceral feminism.

GBV sector worker

Really, we don't need all these commissioners; you just need men to stop killing their women.

Huda Jawad

The feminist founding of refuges, helplines and support centres

Women have always informally provided support and advice to survivors, as well as offering refuges and 'cooling-off' spaces in their own homes for friends, family and neighbours. A fundamental driving force of feminist movements in Britain in the 1970s was the push to build more robust infrastructure that would address gender-based violence, and provide relief from it. This led to the formation of the first domestic violence refuges, Rape Crisis centres and other more formalised support services for survivors. In 1971, a women's liberation group called Chiswick

Women's Aid began protesting against government policies that were affecting families, such as then Health Secretary Margaret Thatcher's withdrawal of free school milk for children over the age of seven. The group marched through the town led by a cow, and were later given a derelict house by the local council at a 'peppercorn' rent that they could meet and organise in. This building would become the first formalised domestic violence refuge in England.[1]

By all accounts, the Chiswick Women's Aid refuge was chaotic and overcrowded. In 1975 it was accommodating about 120 people in a house suitable for thirty-six, confirming the high demand for safe places for survivors of abuse.[2] The Chiswick model provided inspiration for other refuges that were then set up across the country; a loose network of thirty-five such organisations, often funded by jumble sales and coffee mornings, gathered under the umbrella of the Women's Aid Federation England (WAFE) in 1975.[3] WAFE at this point broke away from Chiswick Women's Aid, a move that Chiswick's charismatic and bombastic leader Erin Pizzey responded to with claims that Women's Aid had been co-opted by the women's liberation and gay liberation movements. Pizzey would go on to assert that local authorities should be cautious about funding women's refuges, and would herself glide into 'men's rights' and anti-feminist advocacy.[4]

In 1976, the domestic violence refuge Saheli was set up by a group of South Asian women organising in the local community, who recognised that Asian women fleeing domestic abuse needed safe accommodation. The shift of feminist energy towards developing refuges was both driven by and led to a greater participation of working-class and Black women in what Amina Mama describes as this 'practical political project'.[5] Mama notes that refuge work, and the accompanying close-quarters living of its residents, were a 'powerful test of the movement's anti-racist commitments'.[6] Yet assumptions about women-only refuges being an inherently 'egalitarian' environment were soon exposed to be disconnected from reality. Not only did Black women encounter racism within mixed refuges, but specialist refuges for Black women were provided with less funding per bed space. This inequality in funding between mainstream or 'generic' services and what would later be termed 'specialist' services (those run 'by and for' primarily African, Caribbean and South Asian women) was mirrored by the problems faced by Black women seeking to access housing from local authorities once they were ready to leave, meaning that they ended up spending longer in refuges.[7] These early examples of 'mainstream' services being resourced at the expense of specialist provision set the scene for competition, rather than collaboration. As a GBV sector worker I spoke with describes it, 'When you're in survival mode, then it takes you down a very difficult path which is about competing with your sisters for resources, and also about taking over your sisters, merging with your sisters. So I think it's very difficult.'

It is within this context of resource scarcity that organisations were soon pushed into uneasy collaborations – with the police and other state agencies whose 'law and order' and border enforcement agendas ran contra to the vision of Black feminism – when funding pools were restricted.

While Saheli was being set up, the first Rape Crisis centre was also founded in north London, offering support and advice both in person and via their twenty-four-hour helpline, run by volunteers who sometimes slept overnight in the office.[8] The centres also provided information on reporting to the police and seeking legal action for survivors who wanted to pursue this route.[9] Early on, Rape Crisis workers noted that an unexpected number of their calls were from women reporting historic child abuse, and that the overwhelming number of accounts were regarding rape perpetrated by someone known to the victim (as opposed to a 'stranger'). The centres were clear that women were not obliged to report to the police if they got in touch. Emphasis was placed on the social and patriarchal dynamics of rape, and not on the legal technicalities and medical definitions of rape and its potential impacts – such as post-traumatic stress disorder, first introduced into the *Diagnostic and Statistical Manual of Mental Disorders* (DSM) in 1980 – that were utilised by the police and healthcare institutions. Rape Crisis recognised that sexual violence took many forms, that it wasn't a singular experience for all survivors, and that justice and recovery came in many forms.

Further autonomous Rape Crisis centres were set up across England, Ireland and Scotland in the years that followed (totalling sixty-two centres by 1988), funded by grants from charities and local authorities, and through state funding in Ireland.[10] The political (or apolitical) basis of the centres varied; some broke away from their feminist roots while others remained aligned with the origins of their work. Some of the centres also campaigned on issues that affected survivors, alongside delivering public education programmes to professionals, and submitting evidence to parliamentary advisory groups.

The anti-violence movement's shifting relationship with state racism

In 1971, radical feminists in New York had organised a 'speakout' on rape in a church. Many histories of feminism mark this

as a watershed moment in the origins of the anti-rape movement. While it is true that radical feminist organising in the
1970s forced the topic out into the wider public realm in a new
way, it is also the case that sexual violence had for centuries been
experienced and articulated as a mechanism of terror and control
by Black women in particular, in contexts of colonialism, as a
weapon in wars waged by US and European powers, and during
transatlantic slavery as a tool of oppression and white wealth
creation. The anti-rape movement that emerged in Britain and
the US in the 1970s did not tell that story, instead reading from
the same script that saw the fundamental divide as one between
(white) women and men.

It is not only Black women who were and are harmed by
such a focus. In 1975, Susan Brownmiller published *Against
Our Will*, which quickly became a landmark text on rape. It is
a deeply racist book, which repeats and reinforces stereotypes
about Black male sexual aggression. In her 1981 book *Women,
Race and Class* Angela Davis reflects on Brownmiller's analysis
of high-profile cases where Black men have faced rape allegations, noting, 'In pretending to defend the cause of all women,
she sometimes boxes herself into the position of defending the
particular cause of white women, regardless of its implications.' [11]

For example, when Brownmiller writes about fourteen-year-
old Emmett Till, who was lynched in 1955 after a white woman
called Carolyn Bryant accused him of whistling at her (a claim
she later revoked), she states that Till 'had in mind to possess
[Bryant]', and that Black men (and presumably boys) were
inclined to default to sexual violence because other expressions
of male supremacy – those that are reliant on wealth such as the
accumulation of consumer goods and property – are outside
their purview. [12] Brownmiller sees Blackness as imbued with

an inherent unrefined aggression that is uniquely a product of Black poverty.

Despite sometimes overlooking the inherent racism of policing, the feminists of this era didn't necessarily trust the police. In her history of the Rape Crisis movement, academic Alison Diduck notes that the police were initially hostile to the Rape Crisis movement, refusing to signpost the survivors they encountered to Rape Crisis.[13] In a book written by Met Police inspector Ian Blair in the 1980s, the author lamented that Rape Crisis in London (which the police saw as representing the 'principle voice' of the movement) maintained a consistent critique of the Met Police's handling of cases.[14] Blair had written his book in the wake of Roger Graef's fly-on-the-wall 1982 BBC documentary *Police*, which revealed the extreme levels of retraumatisation that survivors of sexual violence experienced when reporting to the police, and the culture of disbelief which existed within the institution. Outside London, Blair attributed low rates of police referrals to Rape Crisis to the police's lack of confidence in the experience and capacity of the women delivering services, and pointed to 'suspicion and antipathy' on both sides.[15] Blair anticipated that the growth of the Rape Crisis network of centres in Britain was likely to be slow in comparison to its US counterparts, as 'rape crisis centres are now competing for a diminishing pool of charitable and government funds',[16] and he suggested that 'differences in philosophy' between police and feminist organisers were likely to prevent any growth at all.

Over time, the direction of Rape Crisis centres leant towards centring the medicalised trauma of sexual violence. As academic Rachel Loney-Howes writes, there was a 'shift away from the radical claims of gender inequality towards ... the "interiority" – or personalization – of violence'.[17] Acts of sexual violence became detached from their context, moved away from back-drops of social, political and economic injustice where campaigns of violence, including those perpetrated by the state, were both a locomotive and a consequence of inequality. At the same time, allegations of rape also set the dogs of the state (police, prison officers and border guards) upon, typically, men from marginal-ised communities without attempting to disrupt cycles of harm.

Municipal feminism in a time of neoliberalism

With the election of Thatcher in 1979, political life in Britain took a dark turn. Her key policies involved strengthening the rule of law and national defence, increasing spending on police and the criminal-legal system,[18] suppressing trade unions and slashing benefits for strikers, pushing for a leaner welfare state, selling off council housing stock while hiking council rents, and tightening immigration controls.[19] Building on the 1971 Immigration Act that had imposed incredibly tight immigra-tion controls, the British Nationality Act 1981 placed the onus on a sizeable demographic of Commonwealth citizens already living in the country to register as British. It wasn't made clear why registration was necessary, and the fee was a disincentive to doing so.[20] This legislative mess sowed the seeds for the recent 'Windrush scandal' in which Caribbean elders discovered that they could not prove their citizenship. This precarity in immi-gration status, codified into the 1981 Act, redoubled women's oppression by the state: the intensified threat of immigration enforcement action would work to keep women trapped in cycles of poverty and violence.

Black women's health and housing activism emerged in response to the rising social inequality promoted under

Thatcherism, as academic Jenny Douglas writes: 'While black women were expected to be cleaners, nurses and auxiliaries in the NHS, the health needs of black communities were not acknowledged or indeed addressed.'[21]

Into the 1980s, Black women, many of whom were working in healthcare, took action to raise awareness of their communities' health needs. They used their knowledge of, for example, sickle-cell anaemia and Black women's mental health to build support groups and campaigns to raise awareness, and to develop better policies and guidelines for healthcare professionals.[22]

In 1981, the pain and frustration of grinding inequality and daily abuse such as the use of 'sus' laws to harass and arrest young Black people boiled over into riots. A report by Lord Scarman concluded that 'racial disadvantage and its nasty associate, racial discrimination', were responsible for the scenes of rioting. Recommendations from the Scarman report included better police training and efforts to diversify the police force. In a handwritten note to Home Secretary Willie Whitelaw, Thatcher pushed back against these moves for reform, commenting, 'I'm afraid the report seems highly critical of the police.'[23]

The hyper-criminalisation of Black communities and the stigma attached to having served a custodial sentence often left Black men leaving prison with nowhere to live. Black boys who experienced discrimination in education and faced unemployment after leaving school were also prime targets of sus laws that compounded their likelihood of facing homelessness. Black housing and homelessness organisations stepped in to provide advice centres and temporary accommodation, and women were often instrumental in the formation of these services. For example, Camden Black Sisters set up a parent and teacher's organisation that started a housing association called Odu Dua, in recognition of the evident pipeline between institutional racism in education, policing and homelessness.[24] Around forty Black-led housing associations were set up in the years after the riots.[25]

This era of policing is epitomised by the increased use of a 'paramilitary' approach. For example, Thatcher backed the police in their physical attacks on striking miners. After one particular incident – what became known as the Battle of Orgreave – in which South Yorkshire Police violently assaulted miners who had gathered to picket a coking plant at Orgreave in Rother-ham, Thatcher commended the 'magnificent police force well trained for carrying out their duties bravely and impartially'.[26] Despite attempts by the state and mainstream media to discredit and suppress the strikes, Black workers and grass-roots groups organised by communities who were themselves familiar with being targeted and attacked by the police offered political and material solidarity to the miners. These included Lesbians and Gays Support the Miners (LGSM), a collective of queer people who came together after the 1984 Pride march in London to offer support and to raise a strike fund, and the Black Delegation to the Mining Communities (BDMC), which included Black feminist groups such as Southall Black Sisters, Black Women for Wages for Housework, King's Cross Women's Centre and the Southall Monitoring Group. On one occasion, BDMC members travelled in a coach to Kent, taking home-cooked Indian dishes for the striking miners and joining the picket in solidarity.[27] Writing in *Race Today* at the time, co-founder of New Beacon Books and the Black Parent's Movement John La Rose remarked that

> no single battle of the working class and people in Britain has aroused so much passion and attracted so much solidarity from

black workers and unemployeds [*sic*] as the one-year old [sic]
Miners' Strike. What has struck us and won our admiration has
been the courage, determination and heroism of the miners and
their families, especially the women in their organisations.[28]

Social movements resisting Thatcherism posed a challenge to
this form of governing: writing in 1980 for *Marxism Today*, Ian
Gough proposed that 'the women's movement is now a force
capable of resisting some of the more overt attempts at a "back
to the family" approach'.[29] As this new political era was ushered
in, some London-based women's organisations received a sur-
prising influx of financial assistance. The authors of *The Heart
of the Race* note that this increase in cash support was part of
a response at state level to the Scarman report: a 'mass injection of State funds into the deprived areas where Black people
were living' which invigorated a number of welfare projects,
self-help groups, Black women's centres and police monitoring
committees.[30]

A recognition of state-imposed social and infrastructural
inequality wasn't the only reason for the flow of funds into
feminist groups in the early 1980s. One of the key sites of institutional opposition to Thatcher came from the leftward political
shift of the Greater London Council (GLC). The GLC was an
administrative government body that had been set up in 1965
to try and improve planning and spending decisions at a local
level, through organising London and its surrounding regions
into borough councils. The GLC was responsible for roads,
public transport, housing and leisure services, and its overall
purpose was to improve the well-being of Londoners, and to
encourage social, economic and physical development. In 1981
the GLC elected Andrew McIntosh from the Labour Party as its

leader, who was promptly replaced by Ken Livingstone after an internal leadership reshuffle. Livingstone's leadership created great consternation for the governing Conservative Party, who were wary of Livingstone's unequivocally socialist politics, and dubbed him 'Red Ken'.

Speaking at the Scottish Conservative Conference that year, Thatcher commented that the GLC would 'impose upon this nation a tyranny which the peoples of Eastern Europe yearn to cast aside'.[31] Livingstone's GLC made its opposition of Thatcher's government and the neoliberal Conservative status quo evident, slashing public transport costs under the 'Fares Fair' scheme (until the GLC was taken to court and forced to raise prices again); aligning itself with the international campaign for Wages for Housework; investing in nurseries, some of which we were co-operatively run; expressing its support for nuclear disarmament; promoting community-led arts and culture; championing LGBT rights, workplace democracy and community-controlled development; and funding organisations working on issues such as anti-racism and gender-based violence.[32] The work of the GLC under Livingstone has been described as an 'experiment' in urban economic development; even detractors of the last years of the GLC recognise that it was expanding how city planning could operate and which demographics it would prioritise in its spending.[33]

Crucially for feminist movements in London, the GLC set up a well-resourced Women's Committee, and similar committees were also set up in other cities across the UK, largely by Labour councils, reaching thirty-two committees nationwide by 1989.[34] The GLC's Women's Committee was chaired by Valerie Wise from 1982, and had a budget of £16 million and a staff of ninety-six by the mid-1980s.[35] Reflecting on her role as head of equalities and grants monitoring in the committee, Linda Bellos (who would, decades later, join transphobic campaigns in support of anti-trans law-making) explains that the committee didn't just seek to fund the 'usual suspects'; her job entailed actively assisting inexperienced organisations to write funding applications in order to 'get the money out of the building'.[36] Some organisations emerged as a direct result of GLC financial support: Southall Black Sisters set up the Southall Black Womens's Centre in 1983; Claudia Jones Organisation was founded (and continues to provide services for African and Caribbean women and their families in east London); and Rights of Women, which still provides legal assistance to women, was able to employ its first workers.

Of course, the GLC and the Women's Committees were imperfect, and considerable scholarship has examined their flaws. White women's organisations sometimes added Black feminist organisations into funding bids at the 'last minute' in order to secure Women's Committee funding, a practice that would replicate itself across the decades that followed.[37] The committees themselves were also hampered by financial, bureaucratic and ideological blockages from within their own councils. Writing in 1989, Sue Lothian, who had been a women's officer in Edinburgh District Council in the 1980s, reflected on the complexity of 'reconciling theory with reality'; however, she concluded, 'The choice is not between feminising local government and betraying all feminist principles by being coopted wholesale; rather it is about selecting forms of action that will advance women's interests as broadly, and at the same time as specifically, as possible.'[38]

The funding opportunities presented by the GLC undeniably changed the landscape for women's organisations, marking a new

era of 'municipal feminism'.[39] In this era, some feminist organisers took up paid positions in local government and worked 'in
and against' the state in order to leverage public sector resources
to address inequality, while at the same time pushing back against
the hierarchical and patriarchal structures of local government
bodies.[40] Some academics and historians have disputed whether
these 'municipal' feminists can be considered part of the 'feminist
movement'. In 1991 social movement theorists Donatella della
Porta and Mario Diani suggested that for a group of people
to constitute a movement they had to exhibit 'conflictual relations with clearly identified opponents', be connected by 'dense
informal networks' and share a 'distinct collective identity'.[41]
I'm not sure that it's useful to approach feminist history this
way – we cannot learn from our history if we try and overlook
its less 'radical' or more bureaucratic expressions. The pursuit
of social change does not take a 'one-size-fits-all' approach, and
many social movements have pushed for change by working
inside and outside state structures – organisers are not one-
dimensional actors who only work within one specific location
in one particular mode. As academic Freya Johnson Ross notes,
municipal feminism is perhaps better understood as part of a
'constellation of approaches'.[42]

    In any case, municipal feminists brought their politics to
the table and pushed for the resourcing of grass-roots groups.
While there was naturally an overlap between feminists in the
WLM and individual women who were employed in Women's
Committees, it should be noted that there were also sites of
divergence. Freya Johnson Ross's research suggests that the idea
of municipal feminism constituting a wholesale 'institutionalisa-
tion of the WLM' overlooks the ways in which some feminists
had no interest in the machinations of local government, and

the way in which others in the WLM (potentially the majority) were both reliant upon bureaucratic state systems and involved in grass-roots activism in order to improve women's material conditions by any means necessary.[43]

At the same time women were squatting buildings and opening women's centres and other community spaces, the GLC also funded the construction and ownership of whole buildings for feminist organisations. From the viewpoint of the 2020s, when groups and organisations scrabble for meeting places, or for a few desks in a workspace, this feels particularly utopian. My old workplace, Tindlemanor, near London's Old Street, was originally bought and refurbished by a collective of women's organisations including WAFE, London Women's Aid, Lesbian Line and Rights of Women, using a grant provided by the GLC, and its offices are still rented solely by women's organisations to this day.

The Women's Research and Resources Centre (which would become the still-operating volunteer-run Feminist Library) and A Woman's Place, a feminist collectively run resource and information centre which wound down in 1986, were also housed at the GLC-owned Hungerford House on Victoria Embankment, paying only a 'peppercorn rent'.[44] The Jagonari Asian Women's Centre – set up by Bangladeshi women in London's Whitechapel, and designed by Matrix, an all-women group of architects – was built using a £600,000 grant from the GLC, and operated until 2015.[45] The Women's Resource Centre (which still exists as a capacity-building organisation for the GBV sector), which came out of the Women's Education Group at the Institute of Education in London, was also set up in 1983 using GLC funding. Likewise, the East London Black Women's Organisation (ELBWO) was one of the last groups to be funded by the

GLC in 1986, and was set up by Ama Gueye, Hallim Thomas and Mabinte Cyrus after an OWAAD conference, and provided education, training, welfare and leisure facilities for Black women and children in the area. Access to physical spaces for feminists was transformative.

This change was not always for the better, and in order to meet funding requirements many organisations pivoted away from their more feminist and collectivist organising methods. Often this new direction is couched in the language of urgency and pragmatism, suggesting that feminist theory represented 'pie in the sky' ideas that slowed down or held back the fast-paced work of delivering services. In 1983, Sandra Horley took the reins at Chiswick Women's Aid, bringing the organisation into a new era of expansion and professionalism. She later reflected that, in her job at a shelter in Wolverhampton prior to her directorship at Chiswick,

> I walked into the refuge on the first day with an armload of feminist books and my feet didn't hit the ground for five years ... I never read one of those books. All the theory in the world wasn't going to help me deal with what I did.[46]

The availability of funding meant that organisations could expand and take on paid staff, which led to the 'professionalisation' of groups in order to meet their obligations as employers. Organisers at BBWG faced internal disputes over whether to seek funding:

> [BBWG] took a fierce stance on financial independence. We categorically and unanimously refused external funding. Being aware of the yoke that funding could impose on independent political

activism we did not want to be co-opted by the state or voluntary bodies ... since we were not a service-providing organisation we did not require very much financial assistance. Where necessary, we fundraised for our needs through the sale of our newsletter at times, or books or having socials with food and entertainment.[47]

Another member reflected that when moves were made to begin seeking funding (despite the minuted objections of Olive Morris[48]), this activity soon overwhelmed the group and fundamentally shifted their organising structure, noting,

we became a bloody management committee with workers – we became employers. We stopped doing the things that we used to do, like standing on street corners selling papers – or more usually giving them away ... We had become bloody managers, and this is what happens so often. You know, to get funding you have to meet certain criteria; to meet those criteria you have to adopt certain structures and to a great extent the structures dictate the relationships.[49]

Some feminist organisations saw the Livingstone leadership era of the GLC as a period when they had more say in decision making. Members of OWAAD recall feeling that despite awareness of the limitations that funding might bring, they felt that they had to demonstrate their right to access the resources of the state.[50] At times, this access to state funds was framed as almost a reparative claim on the spoils of empire; an entitlement to the coffers of a country whose wealth and welfare state had been built, and was continuing to be maintained, at the cost of blood and toil.

The influx of workers into the GLC from activist backgrounds meant that it was pushed in a progressive direction. The GLC funded the Southall Monitoring Group in 1983, which monitored the violence of policing. As a result of this, an intelligence officer stated in a report that the GLC had set up SMG as a 'political cell' in order to 'undermine the police' and, in the context of a general strike, potentially spread 'widespread destabilisation'.[51] However, OWAAD members reflected that the influence went in both directions:

> our voices were being heard more ... suddenly we had women from OWAAD sitting in County Hall, so people's attentions and energies were being diverted ... some women decided to take those jobs [at race and gender equality units] on, and once it became their job, their paid work, they suddenly had a stake in the system.[52]

Funding was not provided to all women's organisations, and OWAAD members attribute their shutting down in 1983 in part to the 'divide and rule' that this effected, with organisations who framed their work as 'cultural or ethnic' as opposed to 'political' being more likely to garner financial support.[53] In an oral history project held by the British Library which collects stories from the feminist movements, Margaretta Jolly reflects that a certain level of hostility crept into the movement, due to 'competition to attract limited funding, political opportunities, past traumas, and the psychology of social movements that magnify expectation and disappointment ... the competitive impulses that attach precisely to those closest to us'.[54] This element of competition misdirected organisers' attention away from their shared struggle, as they were overwhelmed by the immediate issue of keeping their doors open and their employees' salaries paid. The co-authors of *The Heart of the Race* note,

Increasingly, the effect of state funds on our community has been to
neutralise its militancy; political mobilisation has come to be seen
as a salaried activity. A whole generation of 'ethnic' workers and
race relations experts has been born who are accountable not to the
Black community but to the State which pays them. Their brief,
however unwitting, is to keep the lid on the cauldron, and their
existence is seen as proof of the government's 'concern' to soften
the effects of its own institutionalised racism.

Organisations' ability to continue defining their own priorities
was now weighed up against the benefits of receiving funding.
OWAAD members realised that groups who didn't want to
keep pouring energy into time-intensive fundraising efforts that
raised only small amounts had to 'tweak' their objectives if they
wanted to capture funders' attentions, which handed control
over to the state.[55] This political 'chilling effect' is described by
activist and essayist Arundhati Roy in her 1998 book *The End of
Imagination* as the 'NGO-ization of resistance'. Roy is writing
about the NGO–industrial complex in India, but locates this
NGO-isation in a context of neoliberalism. She suggests that
by providing a salve to the ills of capitalism (for example by the
provision of refuges, helplines and other support services), and
by providing wages to people who might otherwise be activists
in resistance movements, NGOs both 'defuse political anger' and
'turn people into dependent victims'.[56] In the highly securitised,
policed and privatised context of neoliberalism, activists' capacity to participate in resistance movements is severely limited by
climbing rents, crackdowns on squats and the stripping back
of the welfare state: waged work for local authorities or in the
'charity sector' presents a viable alternative.

Rape Crisis centres also changed their governance structures in this period. In her history of anti-rape activism, academic Rachel Loney-Howes notes that some centres felt pushed to water down their politics in order to keep favour with the state, and took on a 'more business-like approach in structuring'.[57] Jane Grant also notes that Rape Crisis centres experienced issues when it came to trying to get funding for services run by women, and that for organisations who refused to abandon their feminist roots in exchange for more reliable financial support, the work of fundraising came to 'predominate over other aspects of the centre's running, both for the paid workers and the collective'. Grant found that Rape Crisis centres took one of two directions: either expanding, professionalising and working with the police and social services, or remaining a small collective and attempting to weather the choppy waters of precarious project funding.[58]

The new model created a clear distinction between 'service providers' and 'service users'. Rather than women organising themselves and supporting each other, they became the helper and the helped. It is not hard to see how this often unfolded into a victim–saviour binary, where anti-violence workers' expertise and knowledge was recognised through their wage, and survivors were characterised within the frame of their victimhood. Rape Crisis centres that resisted this 'professionalisation' were viewed unfavourably by institutions and funding bodies. Instead, funders looked towards organisations such as Victim Support, a depoliticised support service for survivors and witnesses of 'crime' set up by a police officer and a probation officer, which focused on criminal-legal responses to violence. Victim Support worked closely with the police, and began to branch out into support for survivors of sexual violence. In 1979 they began receiving Home Office funding, and by the late 1980s every county in England and Wales had at least one local Victim Support scheme.[59]

In Diduck's history of the Rape Crisis centres, she also notes that another outcome of Roger Graef's documentary *Police* was the establishment of the first sexual assault referral centre (SARC), initially funded by the police and the National Health Service (NHS)[60]. SARCs work with legal models of rape – like Victim Support, their activities are not rooted in a feminist understanding of the dynamics of power and control – and are intended to guide survivors towards criminal-punishment 'resolutions' to their experiences. Despite the evident expertise they held, Rape Crisis were not consulted on the formation of SARCs, and, in the decades that followed, government funding would shift away from Rape Crisis centres and towards SARCs – away from feminist grass-roots organising and mutual aid, and towards criminal 'justice'.[61]

From a committee to a 'sector'

In 1986, despite popularity among Londoners,[62] the GLC was abolished by Thatcher's Local Government Act, and the 'shower' of grant funding came to an end.[63] It was the dissolution of the largest single funding source for women ever established in Britain.[64] By the end of the 1980s, the funding landscape looked perhaps as barren as it had at the beginning of the decade. Some women's organisations that had been reliant on GLC funding closed. Reflecting on materials produced by the Women's Committee, now archived by the Glasgow Women's Library, academic Lucy Brownson found that queer, disabled, migrant, working-class, Black women and women of colour were among those who 'most acutely felt the fallout from the

GLC's abolition, and whose lives have been disproportion-
ately affected by the rampant moralism and nationalism that
Thatcher's government enshrined in law'.[65] Grant presciently
noted in 2001 that 'women's organisations have never had such
sympathetic and generous funders since.'

Some have described the closure of the GLC and Women's
Committees nationwide as a death knell for feminism in the
1980s. Amrit Wilson notes that the legacy of GLC funding was
far from benign, writing that 'it was the state which in the 80s and
90s had established and empowered patriarchal leaders within
communities of colour'.[66] Groups that did survive the GLC
closure, or were set up shortly after, were forced to adopt more
corporate structures and financial models in order to stay afloat.
These would formalise as a 'sector' in order to attain credibility
in the eyes of the business-minded state, so that they could keep
their doors open. Conservative moves towards 'managerialism'
in the public sector – with its strict performance indicators,
emphasis on cost-cutting, short-term contracts and league tables
to encourage competition – also pushed women's charities to
begin quantifying the impact of their work and demonstrating
'value for money' for their services. Concerns had also been
raised within government that charities were unregulated and
evading scrutiny, and so the Charities Act 1992 introduced obligations for registered charities to file annual accounts. Groups
that could not meet funding requirements, or the increasing
obligations placed on them by the state, folded.

The ideology which flourished under Thatcher imparted a
seismic reconfiguration of the social and political landscape.
The ice-cold, scarcity-driven individualism of the 1980s planted
deep seeds which would quickly sprout. Thatcherite rever-
ence for spiritual and emotional doldrums arguably led to the

incorporation of a whole raft of reactionary ideologies into some feminist groups' work. The feminist movement continued to encounter a combination of multiple overlapping problems: in some cases an insufficient analysis of race and class along with the unaddressed impact of trauma and burnout, both in the context of the decimation of the material conditions which had previously enabled radical organising to flourish. With Thatcher came the end of the post-war welfare state; relative access to affordable housing (including more scope for squatting) was destroyed, and the previously vibrant trade union movement was hugely weakened. As Lola Olufemi described to me, 'In the 1970s, there were, before their complete demolition by Thatcherism, certain conditions that were perhaps more conducive to the creation and long-term sustenance of grassroots networks and organising. Organisers during this period benefitted, even indirectly, from free education, welfare state provision, a lower "cost of living", the availability of council housing, and from loopholes in squatting law. There were really, I think, conducive conditions to being able to dedicate your time and your life to organising in that way that doesn't exist anymore.'

Out were the years when local government was funding groups for gay and lesbian communities, and in was a riptide of moral panics, buoyed up by policies such as Section 28 of the Local Government Act 1988, which prohibited the 'promotion of homosexuality' by local authorities, and banned schools from teaching about 'the acceptability of homosexuality as a pretended family relationship'. Thatcher's attempts to sweep queer British life under the carpet also extended to her approach to the HIV/ AIDS crisis in the 1980s, when she advised ministers not to mention 'risky sex' in information campaigns, as she thought it would encourage people to 'experiment'.[67] Interconnected with this lurch towards draconian social attitudes, and the dramatic dip in living standards for working-class people, Thatcherism also engendered a psychic shift – a doubling down of British stoicism as encouraged through her rhetoric of pragmatism. In her 1979 manifesto she had concluded, 'Most people, in their hearts, know that Britain has to come to terms with reality. They no longer have any time for politicians who try to gloss over the harsh facts of life.'

Governance feminism in an age of 'New Managerialism'

In Hugo Young's *Guardian* obituary for Thatcher in 2013 he wrote that her leadership fostered a 'mood of tolerated harshness'.[68] Young speaks to the implantation within the British psyche of a belief that while life may be tedious, grinding, under-stimulating and filled to the brim with discomfort, there is something moral or commendable in not demanding more, for example through collective bargaining; through striking; through popular unrest; through queering love, lust and family models; and through otherwise defying normative structures that enforce inequality. It was Thatcherite neoliberalism as pushed through the meat-grinder of British cultural emotional avoidance.

If the 1980s had been a time of beefed-up crime budgets and violent police confrontations with anyone challenging the neo-liberal status quo, the 1990s saw a consolidation of the 'law and order' brand of British politics. In this decade, both the Labour Party and the Conservative government (led by Tony Blair and John Major respectively) jockeyed to be perceived as being 'toughest' on crime as part of a desperate claim for political ground. The 1990s also marked the beginning of a new era of policing, as the private policing sector – private security guards and surveillance companies, the delivery of technology products and services to the police, and so on[69] – expanded in step with increased attention to the idea of private property.

In theory, the powers of private police do not differ from the powers of the general public; they are able to make 'citizen's arrests' if they are able to justify these actions to a court of law. Yet Crown Prosecution Service guidance notes that under criminal law the 'reasonable' use of force is permitted to defend oneself, another person or property, or to prevent crime, and in particular notes that prosecutors must take 'special care' when considering cases involving non-police individuals who have a 'duty to preserve order and prevent crime'; specifically, this includes private security guards, including nightclub bouncers.[70] When private security guards kill, like police, they are not held accountable: in 2006, three security guards killed Jimmy Mubenga, whom they were attempting to deport on a British Airways flight, and were cleared of manslaughter charges.[71] Acting as gatekeepers to a range of ever-privatised spaces such as airports, nightclubs, hospitals, schools, office blocks and shopping malls, private security guards ensure a level of compliance from the public in response to their demands and intrusions.

Private and public policing meshed together in the 1990s to create a web of surveillance and social control, along with an increase in 'police-generated' crime: more penalisation and criminalisation of activities that would otherwise have proceeded 'victimless', including survival 'crimes' such as skipping a train fare or shoplifting.[72] The narrative of 'policing by consent', characterised by the image of a plodding but fair local policeman on the beat, were conclusively undone in this decade. Police forces were restructured into bureaucratised specialist departments, some of which were tasked with undercover policing, and would infiltrate organising groups and families campaigning for justice, with some cops deceiving women into intimate and sexual relationships.[73] The police were used to crush the dissent of social movements and working-class communities, adopting paramilitary tactics and equipment.[74] In step with neoliberalism, policing shifted to a focus on managing 'risk' in society.

'Risk' was also a key component of approaches to gender-based violence in the 1990s, where 'managerialism' became a defining characteristic of the ever more professionalised feminist movement, a vocal chunk of which by now had shifted into the GBV 'sector'. As the new millennium dawned, a new framework for assessing the 'risk' of domestic abuse emerged: the Multi-agency Risk Assessment Conference, or MARAC. The first MARAC was held in Wales in 2003, and the model has since been replicated across the UK by the domestic violence charity Safelives, as well as internationally. The MARAC brings together a range of agencies such as police, probation, local authority support workers, and health and housing professionals. As Camille Kumar explained at a talk in 2014, 'The reality of the MARAC … is increased surveillance of working class, migrant, and BME populations; MARACs, for many survivors replicate the very same power and control dynamics that they are seeking to escape.'[75]

MARACs have been criticised for the level of information-sharing (in some cases without the consent of survivors), and survivors' decentralisation in decision-making processes: referrals to these multi-agency conferences can be made without survivors' consent.[76] Crucially, MARACs are funded by the Home Office and chaired by police. In 2018, SBS and the civil liberties charity Liberty launched a super-complaint about data-sharing between the police and the Home Office, in their written submission noting that the immigration status of both the victim and the perpetrator had been 'raised repeatedly' during MARACs, with deportation of either party suggested as remedies to the domestic violence the survivor was facing. Their submission also noted a 'a high level of deference to the police as law enforcers' within these conferences. Evie Muir, a former GBV sector worker, explains that 'because of their criminal-legal focus, MARACs measure "high-risk" cases on the basis of available prosecutable evidence as opposed to "genuine need"'.[77] The process also obscures the broader context of harm that interpersonal violence occurs within. One GBV sector worker describes the emergence of individual risk assessment processes, noting, 'We started to do individualised needs assessments, which meant that these particular needs were specific to an individual. And it also meant that we were excusing or pardoning the state in terms of looking at this as an issue of structural inequality.'

The ongoing march of professionalisation in the feminist movement at the same time precipitates a more intimate partnership with the state in order to secure funds and political influence. Black feminist organisations were also pushed to adapt their governance structures in order to keep step with the requirements of running expanded organisations that sought funding to sustain their infrastructure. While SBS and Asha Projects, for example, were initially formed as collectives, the introduction of layers of management to upskill growing staff teams pivoted organisations towards a more 'hierarchical staffing structure'.[78] In her 2001 study of governance in the 'organised women's movement' in the UK, Jane Grant notes that

SBS held on tenaciously to their collective structure and only finally relinquished it in October 1998 to move to a modified or 'democratic hierarchy', with joint co-ordinators, to give greater support and structure ... they were afraid that they would no longer be able to attract women to devote the same amount of time and commitment to the collective as they had given over the years.[79]

In documenting this rationalisation for introducing hierarchy within feminist organisations, Grant indicates a key fracture between workers and management that would sow discord through this process of professionalisation. While the founders of feminist organisations (former organisers within broader feminist movements) had most to gain through this professionalisation – the highest salaries and the most power and influence – through speaking with workers across the GBV sector it appears that the enjoyment of these benefits is tarnished for the beneficiaries by yearning for a 'golden era' of collective and informal forms of feminist organising. This nostalgia spills over into ageist assumptions that junior staff on lower salaries and with less organisational influence who identify their employment as *work* are not as committed to the struggle, or are somehow less radical in their feminist politics. The impact of management's inability to recognise the power they hold in organisations is incredibly detrimental: workers report high rates of unpaid overtime, low salaries and workplace bullying.[80] Writing in 2001, Grant references Siobhan Riordan's assertion that GBV organisations are plagued with an 'illiteracy with power', noting the irony of this reality for a sector committed to laying bare abusive power dynamics, and noting that in GBV sector organisations power is 'treated as invisible – and for this very reason its abuse becomes more likely, a self-fulfilling prophecy'.[81] For Riordan, when the existence of power dynamics is exposed, the extinguishing of a fantasy of egalitarianism leads to deep hurt and resentment.

From the streets to the courts

As the street movement retreated and professionalised into the women's sector, a swell of feminist battles in the 1990s moved onto the legal stage. Writing in the early 2000s, looking back at the preceding decade, Helena Kennedy QC remarks,

> In recent years feminist activity has focused increasingly on the courts, with a move away from demonstrations and direct activism of the 1970s and early 1980s … The victim's lobby grew out of the women's movement, when feminists threw the spotlight on law's failure to deliver for women, particularly in the area of violence against women.[82]

A series of high-profile feminist legal battles in the early 1990s were led by Black feminists pushing back against the invisibility of their lives within a legal system rigged against them. Initially, not all feminist organisations battling the criminal-legal system were seeking to get a seat at the table of lawmaking: in 1989, Southall Black Sisters led their first campaign in support of a survivor of domestic violence who killed her husband. Kiranjit Ahluwalia had been abused by her husband for a decade, and after experiencing a particularly violent episode of abuse she created napalm by mixing petrol and caustic soda, poured it over him while he slept, and set fire to him. Ahluwalia was initially charged with murder and sentenced to life imprisonment. Southall Black Sisters helped her to provide fresh evidence and appeal the conviction, and in her retrial in 1992 the court accepted a plea of manslaughter based on diminished responsibility due to the impacts of the abuse she had endured. Ahluwalia was given a prison sentence of three years and four months – the length of time she had already served, and so she walked free from the court. Campaigns to defend women who had killed the men who abused them served the vital function of enabling survivors to secure liberation from prison. These battles recognised that, fundamentally, the law was not designed to protect survivors of violence.

Where the law does address acts of interpersonal violence, a certain type of victim is assumed: one who is powerless and without agency, who is perhaps 'saved' by the intervention of a state agency, and who is themselves incapable of harm, let alone murder. It is undeniable that feminists in the 1990s operating from more 'professionalised' organisations worked hard to shine light on the endemic nature of forms of gender-based abuse such as sexual violence. At the same time, they often did this through fighting for tougher and longer sentencing, shoring up prisons as the solution.

Feminist work to 'reform' the law in any direction – whether to provide clarity on the experience of victimhood or on the perpetration of abuse – has not, as Wendy Larcombe notes in her study of falling rape conviction rates, constituted a feminist 'success' story. Writing in 2011, Larcombe explains that despite the legal battles of the 1990s onwards, continuing low conviction rates in many rape cases confirm that law reform is a 'project of questionable value'.[83] Koshka Duff also explained to me how concerted efforts to improve criminal justice responses to rape cases can be understood as, in part, a project of white feminist outrage that emerges in response to 'feeling unprotected from an institution that because of racialisation and class position you associate as "on your side"'. The benefit of hindsight is not the ability to condemn an approach to social change, but instead the ability to learn and plan for the road ahead. Knowing that the tireless pursuit of carceral responses to sexual violence has not led to a corresponding dramatic uptick in prosecutions should lead carceral feminists to abandon the tactic of law reform; knowing that this work has not led to a notable decrease in the issue of sexual violence poses a useful lesson for all of us who are building towards liberated futures.

According to feminist histories, the rape law reforms of the 1990s exacted both judicial and symbolic power. An increase in prosecutions wasn't necessarily the end goal of this legislative battle, and illegalising acts such as rape within marriage was considered important in that it indicated to society that the barometer of social morals and ethics was irrevocably shifting. However, the elevation of 'symbolic power' obscures the reality that there is no empirical evidence to suggest a relationship between how 'criminalised' something is and whether people still perform that activity: harsher sentences do not act as a deterrent to violence and can even act as a 'badge of honour' for those who carry them out.[84]

When people perpetrate harm, they are seldom concerned about either the brutality or the illegality of their actions. What is more, importantly, as impartial as it might market itself as being, the law is not a universal threat among all people equally. Writing in 2014, Heidi Safia Mirza pointed out two key aspects of this shift, which is part of the transition from Conservativism to its rebranded sibling, New Labour. The first is that the site of feminist action was reduced to the realms of adjustments, tweaks and deckchair rearrangements on a sinking vessel; the second is that this takes the form of simply defining 'concepts', irrespective of how these concepts materialise in day-to-day life.[85] With the election of Tony Blair as prime minister, feminist discourse shifted from the realm of freedom and liberation to the more institutional framework of 'rights', as the 1998 Human Rights Act passed into law. Notably, New Labour was keen to emphasise that on the flip side of the coin from 'rights' are 'responsibilities', as Tony Blair spoke in 1993 of

> a new concept of citizenship, in which rights and responsibilities go together … As is so clear the more you examine the rise in crime and social disorder in Britain, the problem has been that the Left has tended to undervalue individual responsibility.[86]

The pivot towards 'human rights' was useful only for those who could call on these laws for protection. This is particularly redundant for marginalised groups who are more likely to be cast as the villains of criminal punishment systems, and not seen as the victims.

This managerial and 'professionalised' iteration of carceral feminism of the 1990s took feminism from the streets to the courts, to Parliament and legal libraries, framing violence increasingly as a matter of individual 'risks' as the new millennium arrived. In 1991, rape perpetrated by a person against their husband or wife was made a criminal offence; in 1992 the first independent sexual violence advocate (IDVA) service was set up to support survivors in navigating legal proceedings; in 1996 the Family Law Act introduced restraining orders; and in 1997 the sex offenders' register was set up, while in the same year the Protection from Harassment Act criminalised stalking. These acts of criminalisation represent attempts to concretise, quantify and contain gender-based violence through the pursuit, through the courts, of individual men for individual acts. The very genuine hope underscoring this work is that a retributive, after-the-fact exchange of gender-based violence for prison violence (and its own concomitant context of gender-based violence) will deliver us into a better future. This ideological bedding down occurs in antithesis to Black feminist thought which has long understood the state itself to be a perpetrator of violence. Amina Mama writes that by the 1990s 'the notion of woman as a unitary category was no longer holding sway among activists,'[87] and while the earlier conception of a singular feminist subject that overlooks contexts of race and class was partially dismantled as the twentieth century drew to a close, feminist energies had nonetheless effectively been, and would continue to be, increasingly drawn into criminal punishment agendas. Here we find what Natalie Thomlinson described as a gap between the theory and praxis of well-meaning feminism dominated by the white middle class.

Perhaps predictably, from the late 1980s onwards, feminist work to address gender-based violence that circumnavigated class struggles and bought into the 'law and order' status quo received more mainstream support, both political and financial, than Black feminist organising. An atmosphere of competition for an ever-shrinking funding pool dulled the edge of feminist resistance, at the same time widening the gap between radical grass-roots organising and an ever-expanding charity sector, and successfully co-opting Black women's organisations into state agendas. The digital age ahead would bring new threats and opportunities into the mix, and as the new millennium dawned, the economic backdrop of Britain would experience seismic shocks that starkly laid bare the differences between a feminism that seeks to grab power, and one which seeks to dismantle it.

4

Feminisms of Fear and Resistance
in the New Millennium

Gender-based violence appears as both an alibi for the carceral state and, at the same time, its outcome.

Melanie Brazzell

Back up, back up. We want freedom, freedom. All these sexist, racist men, we don't need them, need them!

Chant at a Sisters Uncut protest, 2015

Criminalisation in the new millennium

Central to carceral feminism are a cast of folk devils: the gangmaster, the terrorist and the pathologically violent classed and racialised man. Naturally, such folk devils require the invention of more criminal offences in order to protect women's safety. As feminists steered new laws onto the statute books, the potential to concretise further forms of harm into laws and to make existing legislation more punitive provided an infinite taskload for feminist organisers, organisations and lawyers. The pursuit of criminalisation is an endless labour, with vast scope for draining time, energy, resource and attention from social movements.

At the level of legislation, the first decade of the 2000s saw feminist involvement in the introduction of a set of laws, civil protections and 'mandatory reporting' policies that placed a legal duty on public authorities to report directly to the police certain forms of violence that are associated with racialised communities. These laws included the Female Genital Mutilation Act 2003, which amended the Prohibition of Female Circumcision Act 1985 by also criminalising the act of taking a girl to another country to perform female genital mutilation or cutting (FGM/C), and almost tripling the length of criminal sentences that could be handed out. This Act was followed a few years later by the Forced Marriage Act 2007, which enabled the serving of forced marriage protection orders (FMPOs) – including without the consent of the survivor – to prevent a person being married against their will and to aid people already in situations of forced marriage.

The question of whether forced marriage should be made a criminal offence had been circulating for almost a decade: back in 1999, a government-organised Working Group on Forced Marriage had been explicit in opposing a criminal offence of forced marriage.[1] Emphasis was instead placed on monitoring and intervention by a range of agencies, including schools, healthcare services, welfare services and the police, with the suggestion made that these agencies had previously been reluctant to intervene for fear of being accused of racism. When the government announced its consultation in advance of the Forced Marriage Act 2007, a number of feminist and GBV organisations made submissions opposing the creation of a new criminal offence. As Southall Black Sisters wrote in their consultation submission,

'Our experience shows that few if any vulnerable young persons are willing to come forward to report a forced marriage if they believe that their parents will face criminal prosecutions and possible imprisonment.'[2]

In this instance, the women's sector was relatively united in pushing for forced marriage to *not* be criminalised; subsequently, civil orders were introduced instead of criminal offences. However, a few years later the coalition government would launch yet another consultation on forced marriage. The consultation findings indicated that 54 per cent of stakeholders were in favour of criminalising forced marriage; consequently, additional criminal offences such as prison time for acts of forced marriage and for breaching FMPOs were imposed through the Anti-social Behaviour, Crime and Policing Act 2014, followed by the criminalisation of breaching FGM protection orders in 2015. This outcome effectively circumnavigated a range of dissenting voices across the women's sector and across the political spectrum.[3] This criminalisation of civil protection orders marked a shift towards what Marianne Hester and Lis Bates describe as 'blurred boundaries' between criminal and civil law through the use of 'hybrid civil–criminal remedies'.[4] The impact of this move towards criminalisation of a breach of a civil order, in combination with survivor's reduced material ability to seek legal redress due to the decimation of legal aid, resulted in a notable dip in applications for protection orders.[5]

A similar move was made in the operation of domestic abuse protection notices (DAPNs) and protection orders (DAPOs): both forms of restraining order which were introduced in the Domestic Abuse Act 2021. These orders can be imposed by the police without the survivor's consent, and breach can result in unlimited fines. Evaluations of previous iterations of these orders noted that survivors often don't report breaches of the orders, which likely occur in more than half of cases.[6] Recommendations were made, including by survivors who spoke to the UK charity Women's Aid, therefore to introduce GPS tracking of people who are subject to the orders.[7]

These recommendations were brought into force with the Domestic Abuse Act, which now gives courts the power to use electronic tagging,[8] despite the fact that tagging and surveillance have always been used to harass and terrorise communities of colour. Tagging technology in particular (the use of GPS ankle bracelets) is a notable additional revenue stream for the private companies that run prisons and detention centres in the UK. Profit making, and the tendering of big-budget contracts, are a huge motivator for the expansion of incarceration and border violence; so much so that the companies providing services to the prison–industrial complex don't even really have to do the work they're paid for. In 2013, outsourcing company Serco had to pay £68.5 million back to the Ministry of Justice after they (alongside G4S, which runs prisons and border enforcement systems globally, and has a 25 per cent stake in the Israeli National Police Academy[9]) were found to have been charging the government to tag and monitor people who were no longer alive.[10]

Other technologies honed by police, such as 'cyber kiosks' which are used to view data (including deleted data) on personal devices, have received pushback from campaigning charities and grass-roots feminist organisers, who describe this process as a 'digital strip search'. Until the system was scrapped in 2020 following campaigns and threats of legal action, survivors who reported rape to the police were being required to sign 'digital data extraction consent forms' which gave police consent to access all their mobile phone data.[11]

These pieces of criminalising legislation built on a number of notions: that forms of violence identified as particularly prevalent in racialised communities are exceptional and pathological in their 'barbaric' and 'savage' nature (this is the racist language frequently associated with forms of abuse such as FGM/C), that in cases of FGM/C and forced marriage there are singular 'victims' and 'villains', and that it is in the survivor's best interest for the person causing harm (often a close family member) to face a criminal prosecution. Naming these forms of abuse 'honour-based violence' implies commonalities around 'why' these violent acts were carried out: that there was something specific, mystic and foreign about these expressions of violence. FGM/C and forced marriage are uniquely associated with 'honour' in the eyes of UK law. At the same time, the murder of women by white men who felt slighted, rejected, or otherwise dishonoured by their own financial mismanagement, for example, wherein the only 'solution' is murder of their whole family, is not deemed 'honour-based'. This double standard reveals tendencies to narrativise violence when located in racialised communities as particularly extreme, monstrous, unthinkable and deserving of the 'full force' of criminal punishment systems and the border regime.

Off the back of these new criminal offences, funding for anti-FGM/C work in the UK briefly flourished;[12] a £1 million budget was made available for a programme run by the Department for International Development (DFID) (part of a £35 million budget ring-fenced for anti-FGM/C work in other countries), and at the height of funding for anti-FGM/C work in 2015 the government was spending £2.7 million on police forces, voluntary organisations, healthcare initiatives and local authority communications campaigns and outreach programmes that were dedicated to addressing FGM/C.[13]

For women's organisations, pitching anti-FGM/C programmes in ways that supported government agendas and narratives became a viable way for them to stay afloat, while organisations such as Imkaan placed clear emphasis on the decline in core funding for specialist organisations that accompanied efforts to criminalise forms of violence such as FGM/C and forced marriage. These organisations identified a shift in the locus of 'justice' against a backdrop of austerity, from community-based organisations who offered specialist and therapeutic knowledge and expertise to the wood-panelled rooms of law courts where a minute handful of 'perpetrators' would be, potentially, handed criminal sentences. In reality, prosecutions for these new 'crimes' were low: the first prison sentence handed out for FGM/C occurred in 2019, thirty-four years after it was first illegalised, and as of 2021, just four convictions for forced marriage had been made.[14] Feminists were encouraged to look to the 'symbolic' power of criminalisation, which requires survivors to testify against their own families and caregivers, while at the same time starving funding from organisations supporting survivors.

The 2010s saw a Pandora's box of potential criminal GBV offences proposed. A bill was put forward to criminalise street harassment; the non-consensual sharing of intimate images was made a criminal offence in 2015 and threats to share such images were criminalised in 2021 with debates on whether to criminalise the consumption of non-consensually shared images and pornographic deepfakes ongoing. Upskirting was made a criminal offence under the Voyeurism Act 2019 after a campaign led by activist Gina Martin, and the Law Commission has subsequently recommended criminalising 'downblousing'. Martin has since reflected on her work, noting that at the age of twenty-five she was acting from a place of hurt and anger, and still journeying into her feminist analysis. She has stated that she became a 'poster girl for carceral feminism', and that her intention is now to work with people to 'prevent this harm outside of existing harmful and racist structures, not with the system to criminalise it'.[15]

It may be true that laws indicate to survivors that the state deems their painful experiences unacceptable. This can be incredibly affirming and important to those of us who have been disbelieved and had our experiences minimised, by parties that might include the state. At the same time, this symbolism fails to prevent these same acts being committed, while funnelling people into the criminal punishment system in order to achieve these 'symbolic' ends. Where radical feminist legal scholar Catharine A. MacKinnon writes about the illegality of, for example, sexual harassment in the workplace as a 'crucial precondition' for the disclosures that emerged from the #MeToo movement over two decades later, she fails to recognise that for survivors who experience forms of violence legitimised and crucial to the state's ordinary functioning – for example when locked up and denied healthcare and legal advice in detention centres, when facing domestic violence and labour exploitation and being met with immigration enforcement, and when being encouraged to 'voluntarily return' after disclosing experiences of workplace exploitation – the fact that other forms of interpersonal violence are in theory unlawful contributes little to their ability to 'speak out'.[16]

Fighting for resources in a time of austerity

The question of resources is crucial to understanding how carceral attitudes find a home in contemporary British feminism.

From 2010, immediately following the financial crash and the public bailout of the financial sector, the Conservative–Liberal Democrat government implemented a policy of wide-ranging public funding cuts. While Chancellor George Osborne announced the 2010 budget with mealy mouthed promises that 'we are all in this together' and that 'everyone will share in the rewards when we succeed',[17] research by the Women's Budget Group and race equality think tank The Runnymede Trust showed that racialised groups and women in particular were more likely to be affected by cuts to benefits and tax credits, as they were more likely to be living in poverty, with dependent children and in larger families.[18] In the first few years of 'austerity', funding for local government was slashed in half, with cuts affecting vast numbers of women, who became more likely to have to provide unpaid care work to fill the gaps in inadequate services.[19] The police had failed to keep women safe from the greedy speculation of investment bankers, whose pursuit of profit was papered over by the government as it channelled funding away from the very public services that women need to stay alive.

Prior to 2008, government departments and local authorities had continued to provide a small amount of funding to women's sector organisations delivering services such as refuge support, as well as helplines, counselling, immigration and family law advice and more. After the financial crash, around half of government funding to specialist refuges for women of colour in the UK was cut.[20] Some specialist services were forced to close their doors, and many others were pushed into uneasy funding arrangements with mainstream organisations who took a largely depoliticised approach and offered more generic support.[21] As funding sources dramatically shrank, emphasis was placed on 'mergers' (more like takeovers from the perspective of specialist organisations) and 'partnership working'.[22] Local authorities began using time-consuming 'competitive-tendering' processes in order to allocate their budgets, which smaller organisations did not have the capacity or skill set to engage in.[23] Consequently, newer, more 'generic' organisations such as housing associations began wading in and scooping up big tenders to deliver anti-violence work and refuges over large geographical areas. According to a report by the Domestic Abuse Housing Alliance (DAHA), by 2021 almost a third of refuge services in England were being run by housing associations and local authorities, instead of by GBV organisations.

Feminist organisations chased the crumbs of available funding, which dragged them away from their organisational and political objectives, and instead saw them pouring energy into work such as lobbying the government to adjust policies and create new criminal offences, offering 'innovative' and tech-based short-term projects, analysing data on prosecution rates, and delivering services which are conditional on survivors engaging with criminal-legal systems. The increasing need for feminist organisations to be operating in close proximity to the government in order to sustain their work, including those led by Black and minoritised women, hollowed out the political centre of the sector.

I spoke with a worker from the GBV sector. She explained, 'The sector really sees itself as dependent upon the resources and funding that the state is able to provide ... Once you start to think like that, then your critique of state policies really starts to disappear.'

There is a tension between the fact that the state (and its funding decisions) holds the keys to the livelihoods of women working in these organisations and, at the same time, the fact that racialised women's experiences of violence are singularly dismissed or exoticised by the state. I spoke with Huda Jawad, co-director of the Three Hijabis, who suggested that against this backdrop, organisations led by Black and minoritised women have at times supported criminalisation of FGM/C, for example, as a form of personal retribution: 'Their solutions are so coming from a place of visceral pain. They are unable to see … that "my lived experiences are being weaponised against whole swathes of people for a separate agenda, and I'm merely just another tool in the patriarchal white man's toolbox of tricks." And so, you know, the role that they play in the othering of women from the global majority, or black and minoritised backgrounds is massive. And in that process, the trauma is not healed.'

Women's organisations have found themselves backed into a corner. The rise of a more politically devoid 'cultural feminism' within these spaces – a feminism concerned with 'diversity' and 'representation' – dovetailed precisely with the rise to power of the UK's second woman prime minister, Theresa May. While on the one hand, from May's time as Home Secretary and through her ascent to 10 Downing Street, grass-roots feminist activity grew in resistance to her white feminist state building, on the other, professionalised feminist organisations sought a seat at her table.

Hostile environments and white saviourism

During her time as Home Secretary (2010–16), Theresa May presided over the expansion of the UK's detention estate through the opening of Morton Hall immigration detention centre in Lincolnshire (now a prison). She also dismissed demands to close Yarl's Wood Immigration Removal Centre despite a Channel 4 documentary detailing self-harm and abuse by guards and the publication by Black Women's Rape Action Project and Women Against Rape of a dossier of sexual abuse allegations against detention guards.[24] During her time in office, May also oversaw a 600 per cent increase in the detention of people from EU countries, and launched the government's 'hostile environment' policy through two successive Immigration Acts, which in practice sought to make life in the UK untenable for racialised communities.[25]

Despite this ghoulish track record, notable feminist charities working on gender-based violence congratulated and welcomed May when she became prime minister in 2016. Alison Phipps reminds us that when May stepped down as prime minister three years later, the white tears she shed at the podium outside 10 Downing Street 'did political work' to wash away her sins, inspiring charities such as Women's Aid to tweet (and delete) gratitude for May's 'efforts' in office.[26] This alignment of the women's sector with one of the key players of neoliberal state building illuminates the hollowing out of the political core in anti-violence work. A vast distance has been travelled, from the radical life-saving activities of feminism's supposed 'heyday' to the present day, where the organisations founded then call for new criminal offences, broker relationships with right wing politicians and vie for policy 'wins' which can be quantified in funding reports.

That Theresa May is a woman, and that she deployed the rhetoric of humanitarianism and feminism around such legislative contributions as the 2015 Modern Slavery Act and the 2021 Domestic Abuse Act, provided satisfactory feminist credentials for some in the mainstream women's sector. A draft version of the Domestic Abuse Act prescribed immigration enforcement as a salve for domestic violence, suggesting that in some cases a survivor 'may be best served by returning to their country of origin and, where it is available, to the support of their family and friends'.[27] While this clause was eventually edited out of the bill, it exposes the underlying intention of the Act, which applies a 'law and order' and 'border control' response to issues of gender-based violence. At the same time, community-based services, including refuges (the term 'refuge' does not appear at all in the 32,000 words of the Act), are pointedly omitted from the government's funding priorities.[28] The Act is one example of the red herring of 'feminist lawmaking'. As bell hooks wrote in the 1980s, reflecting on the appointment of Sandra Day O'Connor to the Supreme Court by Ronald Reagan, 'Individual women can gain power and prestige in the existing structure if they support that structure.'[29] Having 'women's faces in high places' is not a revolutionary end goal.

May was joined in these ranks by a host of women, including Cressida Dick, the former commissioner of the Metropolitan Police (and its first woman commissioner), who entered the police force in the 1980s 'buoyed up by the feminist movement',[30] and Priti Patel, Home Secretary between 2019 and 2022, who devised a whole raft of racist and punitive immigration policies and also identifies with a feminism constitutive of 'the freedom to succeed'.[31] Dick, May and Patel represent almost a totality of state power framed as feminist activity: their efforts encompass sharpening the knives of border enforcement and ramping up the violence of the carceral state and its welfare abandonment, as meted out by police and prisons in the name of women's safety.

The carceral feminist fight against modern slavery

The shining zenith of Theresa May's feminist lawmaking is perhaps her work on modern slavery. Soon after the enlargement of the European Union in the early 2000s – with Cyprus, the Czech Republic, Estonia, Hungary, Latvia, Lithuania, Malta, Poland, Slovakia and Slovenia signing accession treaties in 2004, and Romania and Bulgaria in 2007 – narratives and moral panics around the 'frail, white Eastern European girl victim' began to emerge. The Conservative government capitalised on this concept, and academics from the mainstream feminist movement joined hands with their project, providing spurious research and ideological backing for the relentless and costly pursuit of slavery 'gangmasters' which manifested as the Modern Slavery Act 2015.[32]

The Modern Slavery Act is determinedly a 'law and order' bill which seeks to punish 'criminal gangs' and harness border controls in the fight against human trafficking. The Act was a landmark piece of legislation, although not for the reasons espoused in Home Office press releases. The mid-2010s marked a short period of prolific carceral feminist lawmaking. They saw the further criminalisation of stalking in the Protection of Freedoms Act 2012, the criminalisation of coercive and controlling behaviour in the Serious Crime Act 2015 (with an anticipated additional budget requirement for the criminal-legal system of £19 million[33]), the introduction of the Violence against Women, Domestic Abuse and Sexual Violence (Wales) Act by the Welsh Assembly in 2015, and the first rumblings of a draft Domestic Abuse Bill. The Modern Slavery Act was particularly significant in that it unabashedly crystallised in law the instinct to weaponise prisons and border controls in the name of women's safety.

The issue with 'modern slavery' as a framing, as the former adviser to the UK's Anti-slavery Commissioner Emily Kenway explained to me, is not that the types of exploitation and harm that it outlines do not exist – they absolutely do. However, this legislation performs a series of cognitive tricks that prohibit rather than prescribe safety for survivors, which carceral feminism picked up and ran with from the 2010s onwards. 'Modern slavery' framings individualise labour exploitation and other harms. Experiences of abuse are separated out from a context of structural inequality, glossing over the role of poverty and global inequality as a condition of racial capitalism that pushes people to make dangerous journeys and work in jobs where bosses treat workers abysmally, knowing that they cannot seek redress without immigration enforcement action.

After individualising experiences of abuse, the Act then provides 'remedies' that are heavily weighted towards the criminal-legal system, using the issue of modern slavery as a way to push law, order and border agendas and to expand profit for private companies. Kenway recounted that 'one of the things that comes up with people who are in trafficking situations, in forced-labour situations, is that they want to be working and earning a decent living, often sending remittances home ... So "rescuing" them, extracting them, and putting them in [Home Office] housing is not a very intelligent approach.'

Furthermore, charities report that the vast majority of women going through the government system for identifying and triaging potential victims of trafficking for support – the National Referral Mechanism (NRM) – are being housed in accommodation provided by three private companies (Serco, Mears Group and Clearspring Ready Homes) that are awarded hefty contracts to deliver very poor-quality housing while pouring dividends into the pockets of their shareholders.[34] In these ways, the Modern Slavery Act reinforces the border regime rather than recognising the border as a site of harm that produces danger and exploitation.

Why did feminists so willingly get on board with this deeply flawed legislation? Crucially, modern slavery legislation was also pitched by government as a vital tool in addressing 'the harm and exploitation that can be associated with prostitution'.[35] Mainstream feminism's obsession with 'ending' sex work – reviving the concerns of the bourgeois feminists of the 'first wave' – fits perfectly with those key carceral feminist concepts: fixed and powerless victimhood, gatekept perimeters of womanhood, and the insistent divorcing of experiences of violence from their social and economic contexts. Kenway described the inability of carceral feminism to grapple with the way in which sex workers (and all workers, for that matter) may identify harms within their industry while also having autonomy and expertise about their needs as workers: the ability to say, 'We're agents, and there are problems.'

The loudest voices in mainstream British feminism largely call for the implementation of the 'Nordic model', a legal framework that seeks to criminalise the purchase of sexual services. The Nordic model is currently used in Sweden, Norway, Iceland, France, Ireland, Northern Ireland and Canada, and is shown to be ineffective in 'ending' sex work, while also making conditions more dangerous for sex workers. Fewer clients (decreased 'demand') gives workers less choice over whom they work with and where they work, and means that clients rush negotiations and vetting as they are worried about being noticed by police. In essence, the Nordic model tips the balance of power further in favour of the clients, rather than the workers. Sex worker advocacy groups call instead for the 'decriminalisation' of sex work, ensuring that workers can access the same legal rights and protections as workers in other industries, thereby reducing the potential for exploitation.[36]

The Nordic model and 'end demand' is a crucial campaigning issue for carceral feminism, and is pushed for by small organisations and charities working on issues of gender-based violence with and without explicit 'feminist' stances, and also by politicians across the political spectrum. Elizabeth Bernstein wrote in the late 2000s that similarly in the US, a range of faith groups (buoyed up by Bush-era funding initiatives), activist groups, human rights initiatives and legal instruments similar to the Nordic model coalesce around the mission of 'saving' sex workers from their work, which is not recognised *as* work (because work is framed as 'good' while exchanging sex for money is 'bad'). The explicit focus of the Nordic model is on punishment of those 'demanding' services through payment; harm here is concentrated in the figures of individual men who can be isolated, caught and locked away. Through this lens, the villains who perpetrate harm – the pimp, the punter and the gangmaster – are imagined to always be 'out there', and so border control also becomes a tactic of protection, with violence a potential contagion that must be held at bay. Academic Sara Farris describes this particular expression of carceral feminism as 'femonationalism' – the invocation of women's rights in order to further a racist nationalist agenda, and the forming of ideological convergences between, for example, right wing politicians and neoliberal white feminists.[37] Once more, carceral feminism's obsession with symbolism and morality ignores real-world consequences and fails to address the issues identified by sex workers themselves: the decriminalisation of their work in order to promote access to safety and economic justice.[38]

Anti-terror legislation and the confection of fear

The 'war on gender-based violence' elicits fears of perpetrators who are pathologically evil, cruel and inhuman, an affront to the alleged 'British values' of democracy, rule of law, mutual respect, tolerance and individual liberty. That Britain is singularly responsible for enacting some of the most undemocratic, oppressive and intolerant forms of violence and subjugation on a global scale does not seem to be factored into claims about such values. 'Terrorism' and 'extremism' provided, in the mid-2010s, a conceptual slop bucket of policy in the name of 'security' and counterterrorism. Crucially for women's organisations, along with this policy package came funding for groups that were willing to co-sign this agenda. Money became available through a scheme called 'Prevent', which places a duty on public bodies such as schools and health institutions to monitor and report people to the government, under the guise of 'preventing' people from being drawn into terrorism.

Funding provided to women's organisations under counter-terror legislation through schemes such as Prevent carried implicit and explicit expectations that those organisations would aid surveillance and tacit control of Muslim communities. Research carried out by academic Sam Matthews in 2020 found concerns that Prevent funding had become the 'primary funding source' for organisations run by and for women of colour, including support services for survivors of domestic violence.[39] Huda Jawad describes a certain level of defeatism that comes with accepting this funding: 'There's that kind of analysis that says, "Oh, well, you know, if we are helping women from Muslim communities fight misogyny in their community, then that's fine. You know, that's a win–win, and we got money, and that's fine".'

Unsurprisingly, the integration of Prevent agendas into women's organisations reduces survivors' trust in these services. As Imkaan reports, specialist organisations have been forced to sculpt their direction of travel to suit Islamophobic public policy. As Sundari Anitha and Sukhwant Dhaliwal report, Southall Black Sisters discovered that

> BME community and women's groups were forced to transform the nature of their organisations either by becoming generic services for all women fleeing violence to abide by the terms of new commissioning regimes (that also require organisations to do more for less money) or by establishing Muslim specific programmes in order to attract Prevent or Cohesion funding.[40]

Part of this ever-closer relationship between anti-terror laws and GBV policy and funding is the bundling up of neo-imperial state agendas (to 'crack down' on terrorism through bombing 'democracy' into other countries) with supposed crusades to save Muslim women from the threat of their own communities. The rhetoric used to justify these imperial invasions is overtly femonationalist; as the 'War on Terror' ramped up in the wake of 9/11, Cherie Blair called for interventions against the Taliban in order to 'give back a voice' to women in Afghanistan.[41] Writing for OpenDemocracy in 2020, Amrit Wilson noted, 'As far back as 2006 [Crown Prosecution Service] officials were asserting, without evidence, that terrorism, forced marriage and extremism were all inextricably linked ... But the hollowness of the government's "concern" is evident.'[42]

These linkages play upon racist and orientalist notions of non-Christian faiths having a particular claim to violent forms of patriarchy that are, supposedly, absent from forms of religious or cultural expression that are understood as embodying 'British values'. Within Black and minoritised organisations in the women's sector, these attitudes have in some places become inculcated into organisations themselves, who in turn reject the role of faith and religion in survivors' lives. Huda explained to me, 'There is this … "by and for" secularist mindset that is deeply hostile to the use of faith and religious discourse as an identity marker, and as a way of understanding the world. And so for them, it is described as "fundamentalism", a fight against fundamentalism, rather than an Islamophobic agenda.'

The seepage of Islamophobia into feminist organisations also works to preclude radical solutions to gender-based violence. As Lola Olufemi told me, 'They're saying, "Abolition is all nice and good as a theoretical concept, but actually it doesn't work because the men that we deal with are somehow exceptionally violent." When they say this, they are making a very clear choice to collude with the state in racialising these men, marking them as exceptionally violent, in order to justify increased policing, securitisation and surveillance – all of which harm working-class women. They do so to appease liberal feminists, whose only recourse to end violence is law-making, and who were once their antagonists due to their refusal to recognise how race and gender constitute each other.'

Furthermore, these same organisations, in their 'doubling down' on the victimhood of survivors, detached from the live political context of Islamophobia and its concurrent expressions through border violence and imperialism, at the same time engage in binaried understandings of gender that preclude, for example, trans survivors from the viewfinder of their work. As academic Abeera Khan notes, 'The language and tactics of both transphobia and particularly Western European deployments of anti-Islamic secular hostility overlap in their insistence of the victimisation of these political positions.'[43]

Khan points to the leverage of victimhood as a defence for attacking or abandoning other marginalised groups. This overidentification with the category of 'victim' fortifies the belief that someone who is a victim can, directly or indirectly, do no harm.

The digital realm of repression and resistance

With the increased availability of the internet and technology came surveillance tech and data-driven policing. Police targeted crime 'hot spots' in order to improve the appearance of their 'effectiveness', both creating and confirming crime statistics. Private companies began using tech and data to assist in the confecting and sculpting of crime landscapes. For example, global consultancy firm Accenture provides the West Midlands police with data on 'people, gangs, crime trends',[44] and between 2013 and 2018, Kent police used software developed by US tech company PredPol to enact 'predictive policing'.[45] Restricted reports that were released to the public through Freedom of Information (FOI) Act requests detail that the costly PredPol software assisted Kent police in 'predicting' hair-raising incidents of lawbreaking, such as possession of small amounts of drugs, theft of a wallet and a group of boys being rowdy while fishing.[46] In 2012, in response to the 2011 civil unrest in London, a database of supposed gang members was formed – the gangs matrix – almost 90 per cent of which has comprised racialised people, the overwhelming majority of whom are Black men.[47]

While the police were quick to utilise tech to surveil and harass communities, social movements also benefited from the ability to network people across large geographic spaces. However, differences in comprehension and usage of the internet and tech soon led to generational divides, including within feminist movements. Conversations around usage of and safety within digital spaces would quickly begin to mirror those around safety in the 'real world'. Targets of online abuse would be advised to 'stay away' from social media sites where they faced harassment, paralleling the way in which marginalised communities are blamed for their own experiences of harassment when moving through public spaces, particularly after dark or when alone.

Since the early 2010s, young people have been characterised as being 'disconnected' from real life, as navel-gazing selfie-obsessives who struggle with 'face-to-face' communication. Digital forms of activism associated with millennial organisers were derided as 'clicktivism' and 'slacktivism'. Activism in the forms of 'bodies on the line' and 'marching on the streets' continued to be heralded as a pre-digital 'golden era' form of resistance. The depiction of feminist activism as existing either bravely offline or half-heartedly on the internet reveals the one-dimensionality of a mainstream feminist analysis which fails to recognise the use of social media sites by protestors to share information during popular uprisings. For example, activists' use of social media played a critical role in the seismic pro-democracy uprisings collectively referred to as the 'Arab Spring', and communication on Blackberry Messenger (BBM) by participants in the 2011 civil unrest in London and across cities in the UK enabled the sharing of safe routes and helped people to evade police.[48] In turn, this rhetoric – that the digital realm offers a 'lesser' forum for feminist action – was used to dismiss and erase both the myriad ways in which vast numbers of young organisers were continuing to mobilise, and the ways in which swathes of people less able to 'take to the streets' – due to being disabled or living with chronic illnesses; having caring responsibilities; living in rural and isolated areas; having insecure immigration status or being in an illegalised line of work; and due to the threat of interpersonal, public and state harassment and violence, among other things – were harnessing digital forms of organising, communication and resistance in order to act as political subjects.

The internet also provided new confessional spaces where individual testimonies could be heard and shared widely – not unlike the consciousness-raising groups of the so-called second wave – and digital tools that enabled users to quickly and simply voice political demands. In the UK this capability manifested in surges of internet-based feminist activity, such as the Everyday Sexism Project, which was set up to 'catalogue instances of sexism experienced on a day to day basis' and had reached 100,000 contributions by 2015.[49] The creation of online petition sites brought forth campaigns such as the sex-worker exclusionary No More Page 3, which sought to remove topless photographs of models from page 3 of the *Sun* newspaper. No More Page 3 frequently denounced the fact that the *Sun* encouraged its readers to look at 'boobs over breakfast', pushing for the end of income for the models whose voices were notably absent from the campaign, and overlooking the quotidian sexist, racist and homophobic nature of the rest of the *Sun*'s contents. The pitching of the louche and deviant 'boobs' against the whole-some, family-values–laden, and emphatically British 'breakfast' was representative of a particular strain of 2010's feminist discourse which drew on long histories of bourgeois white women's pearl-clutching fragility, modesty, purity and respectability, weaponised in the name of 'women's rights'. Around the same time, a campaign raised £13,000 to put the author Jane Austen's face onto banknotes, without attempting to improve women's access to banknotes irrespective of whose face was decorating them.

'Anti-pornography' expressions of feminism found a renaissance in the 2010s, including as asserted by feminist commentators who decried a broad range of modes of dress and forms of labour and leisure that younger women were engaging in, from high heels and Playboy-branded clothing to sex work and pole dancing. Working-class women in particular bore the brunt of this chastisement. Pornography was framed as inherently violent and its depictions blamed for harm in society,[50] with the more salient issue of precarious working conditions for porn actors pushed to the margins. In the wake of the murder of landscape architect Joanna Yates by her neighbour, Vincent Tabak, in 2010, co-founder of law reform group Justice for Women Julie Bindel (who would later become known for her transphobic and anti–sex work screeds in mainstream media publications) called for legislation against violent pornography. Her objection was not that Tabak might have sought to re-create scenes from the pornographic images discovered on his laptop after his arrest, but that according to her analysis, 'in order for violent pornography to exist, a woman has to be harmed in its production'.[51]

Doubling down on victimhood

Bindel's analysis speaks to an inclination within carceral and liberal feminism to cartoonify women, depicting them as powerless victims. As Koshka Duff explained to me, reflecting on feminism's historical preoccupation with narrowly defined ideas of 'woman', 'there were some tendencies to talk about "male violence" in a very totalising way that didn't really attend to intersections [of inequality]. This could sometimes fall into quite biological essentialist rhetoric.'[52] An upsurge of gender essentialism in the second half of the 2010s increasingly manifests in violent transphobia and compounds the erasure and dismissal of trans survivors, including attempts to exclude trans communities from support services.

Trans-exclusionary radical feminism (TERF), or 'gender-critical' ideology, is upheld by a small but influential segment of the present-day mainstream GBV sector. Particular attention is paid by those advocating TERF ideology to trans women, whose womanhood is denied, and whose presence in 'women-only' spaces (for all of history) is framed as a (new) threat to cisgender women. Lucy McKay from INQUEST describes the ideological erasure of trans women as the 'plothole' in carceral feminism, given that gender-based violence is perpetrated by people of all genders through dynamics of unequal power. This approach is also based on an idea of the innate victimhood of cisgender women. By this logic, violent men should be policed and locked up in prison, but women who harm should not be policed or incarcerated due to their victimhood. As artist and writer Linda Stupart notes, 'Victim status becomes so central to an understanding of self, that this trauma-identity becomes individualised, paranoid, and exclusionary, and thus weaponised against other (often more) marginalised people.'[53] Stupart explains that this doubling down on victimhood often goes hand in hand with a trans-exclusionary politics, writing, 'Trans-exclusionary women build walls around their womanness in order to retain their primary victim status.'[54]

The dangers of reifying this victim status are illustrated well by a framework called the 'drama triangle', which was developed by psychiatrist Stephen Karpman and others in the 1960s. Ironically, this framework is commonly used by domestic abuse specialists in the women's sector which in Britain plays host to powerful transphobic lobbying voices. The drama triangle (literally a diagram of a triangle) illustrates three potential dysfunctional archetypes that people inhabit when relating to each other in conflict. These roles are victim, persecutor and rescuer. Karpman suggests that most people will have a natural 'starting gate' position, but that we may move around the drama triangle, shifting between the positions of victim, persecutor and rescuer, as we spiral further into conflict without healthy resolution. In the framework of the drama triangle these roles are all dependent on each other: a rescuer requires a victim (and therefore also a persecutor) in order to feel valid and needed, a persecutor needs a victim in order to feel powerful, and a victim is characterised by powerlessness and therefore requires both a rescuer and a persecutor in order to complete their identity, and so on.

The purpose of this framework is to identify dysfunction, and to emphasise the need to 'escape' the drama triangle, to transcend 'roles' and instead shift into authentic behaviours where we recognise our own capacity to act and relate collaboratively. In 1990, counsellor Acey Choy developed the model of a 'winner's triangle', which articulates this opportunity to shift from rigid archetypes towards the use of skills to move through conflict. In Choy's winner's triangle, the victim harnesses the power of their vulnerability and can ask for help and co-create resolutions; the persecutor utilises their assertiveness to solve problems, and the rescuer cares and coaches in a boundaried way, rather than creating bonds of dependency. Carceral feminism's focus on victim status, and the fixed victimhood of cisgender women, alongside the fixed persecutor status of men in general, does not serve any of us. This position also leaves vast swathes of survivors who do not identify as women, or who are excluded by these feminists from the category of 'victim' or 'woman' with nowhere to turn when they experience gender-based violence.

The carceral court of public opinion

The concept of victimhood would inadvertently become a key point of discussion in the late 2010s, with implications for the alignment of ideas around disclosure, justice and carcerality. In 2017, building on the previous work of activist Tarana Burke, in response to a tweet from the actress Alyssa Milano, survivors began sharing their experiences of gender-based violence online using the soon viral hashtag '#MeToo'. The initial media spotlight was largely given to allegations of abuse against film director Harvey Weinstein; however, the movement quickly gathered steam away from the bright lights of Hollywood: its equivalent expressions, such as #YoTambien in Spanish, #BalanceTonPorc in French ('denounce your pig'), and the use of rice bowl and rabbit emojis in China ('rice' and 'bunny' are pronounced mi tu in Mandarin) soon began circulating. The narrative arc of Weinstein's 'downfall' (after a long, glittering and well-compensated career in which he reportedly assaulted at least eighty women) ended in his being sent to prison. The 'solution' posed to the clearly widespread and normalised reality of sexual violence was the 'justice' offered by the criminal-legal system.

While some women's and feminist organisations pushed for a broader harm-reduction approach in response to #MeToo, such as improving media reporting on gender-based violence, and a celebrity-backed fund donated over £1 million to women's organisations providing advice and support to survivors, media coverage of the issue rarely explored the topic of preventive approaches to violence.[55] Calls for 'consequences' from white feminist figureheads often pointed to distinctly carceral solutions. For example, speaking to the *Guardian* in 2018, then Women's Aid CEO Katie Ghose stated that the era of #MeToo presented a 'momentous time' to address gender-based violence, and that 'police just do not have enough tools in their box to keep women safe and to tackle the perpetrators'.[56] In an interview with *Harper's Bazaar*, Labour MP Jess Phillips outlined her hope for the future, that 'the stories of men who kill their wives *and only face three years in prison* and the rape cases *that never lead anywhere* will be a thing of the past'.[57] Phillips shows here the limits of the carceral feminist imagination: that our wildest dreams constitute tougher prison sentences and punishments – the 'eye-for-an-eye' expansion of harm rather than preventive policies or adequate support services or even a world without rape or murder.

The burgeoning twenty-first-century abolitionist movement in Britain, however, presented visions of justice in the wake of #MeToo that were not reliant upon the carceral state. Direct action anti-austerity group Sisters Uncut launched a campaign to stop courts from forcing survivors to hand over huge amounts of personal data, and to demand funding for transformative justice and bystander intervention programmes instead of the criminal-legal system. Black Lives Matter UK shared a pack of resources and readings on masculinities and sexual violence, and urged their followers to begin unpicking the ways in which they benefited from and were protected by gender inequality, tweeting, 'For every #MeToo, there is an #IveDoneThat. Here's a place to learn and unlearn.'[58]

Academics Bianca Fileborn and Rachel Loney-Howes describe the way in which mainstream engagements with #MeToo replicated 'many historically problematic features of public feminism and anti-rape activism'. These features include the inclination to use the legal system as a site of 'individual redress'.[59] While clearly evidencing the endemic nature of gender-based violence, the most vocal and documented proponents of #MeToo as a locomotive for social change fell into the classic traps of white feminism. Familiar stumbling blocks included interpreting a widespread issue as being communally experienced through the universalising lens of women's victimhood only, focusing on the primacy of 'male' violence as the key blockage for liberation while neglecting socio-economic contexts of poverty and border violence that drive and compound inequality, representing 'victim' and 'perpetrator' as distinct and mutually exclusive identities, and locating 'solutions' for violence in the very carceral and neoliberal state that requires the continuation of a landscape of inequality and exploitation in order to exist and continue to accrue profits.

Almost immediately after its upsurge, the #MeToo movement faced significant backlash. Commentators suggested that feminists were going 'too far'; that they were at risk of engaging in a 'witch-hunt' that would ruin men's lives, and of overextending the definition of sexual violence by slinging around accusations of criminal acts in scenarios that were just 'bad sex'. This latter issue is symptomatic of the criminal-legal emphasis on specific definitions of sexual violence and criminalisation of those defined acts, as championed by activists and feminist lawyers in the preceding decades. The possibility – or reality – that many experiences of sexual violence are not a clear-cut action but an amorphous and shifting felt experience informed by context, in many cases identified retrospectively, is incompatible with a criminal-legal system that needs to be able to identify a clear and definite act, a perpetrator and a victim. The issue here is that the criminal-legal system does not seek to understand the causes of sexual violence in order to work towards eradicating it.

In her exploration of the #MeToo movement – in some sense a modern iteration of consciousness-raising within a public forum – Nadine Hartmann draws on the ideas of theorist Michel Foucault to warn of the potential for 'governmentality' to co-opt public disclosures of violence. She notes that neoliberal states cloak their oppressive use of power (e.g. the use of surveillance, police and prisons which prescribe premature death) in the language of freedoms and women's right to 'share their stories' for as long as it is useful for the state's agendas. For Hartmann, this use of power by states is '[a] productive power that encourages us to speak, a power that always addresses the subject in her freedom – and which may very well reward the "silence breakers."'[60]

Academic Alison Phipps similarly writes that these testimonies have the potential to be 'appropriated by punitive (and therapeutic) state governmentalities'. She concludes, 'Solidifying the "truth" of women's experience through "speaking out" ... was not necessarily liberation.'[61] Women who hold power due to their class position – which, as noted by theorist Stuart Hall, is experienced through the 'modality' of race both by communities who are 'racially defined' and those who are not[63] – must reckon with the reality that, most emphatically, their disclosures in particular reify and concretise the ability of the state to further entrench inequality through harassing, surveilling, locking up and otherwise punishing marginalised groups. In the context of the journey of UK feminism into the late 2010s, #MeToo arrived at a time when carceral feminists were primed to scoop up these disclosures as evidence for the need to repair (reinforce) the criminal-legal system and to batten down the hatches of border controls and deportation as a means of protecting women. At the same time, emerging abolitionist groups seized an opportunity to present alternatives to police and prisons; they flexed their imaginative sinews and tested out the possibility of abolitionist ideas in a UK context.

As the 2020s dawned, the fissure in contemporary feminism was acutely felt. When Sarah Everard was murdered by police officer Wayne Couzens, the feminist organising group Reclaim These Streets planned to hold an emphatically socially distanced and masked vigil on Clapham Common, near where Sarah was abducted. The organisers faced pushback from police who said that the vigil would be banned as it was 'unlawful' under lockdown restrictions – aptly, the same laws that Couzens had used to abduct Sarah – and organisers were told that if they continued to plan the vigil they could be prosecuted for 'conspiracy to commit a crime'. Reclaim These Streets cancelled their vigil, and an organiser with Reclaim These Streets spoke on national television in defence of Met Police commissioner Cressida Dick, who was facing calls for her to step down, decrying the idea of a 'pile-on'.[63] Sisters Uncut, a group that emerged during the first years of austerity in the 2010s to protest cuts to women's services and had long mounted a critique of the state and the police, went ahead with the vigil. Cressida Dick ordered the police to clear the vigil, resulting in scenes of violence against stricken mourners. A member of the group would remark a year later,

The police are perpetrators of violence. We saw this in the way they beat women at Clapham Common last year, we saw it in the murder of Sarah Everard, and we've seen it in the countless reports of police sexual abuse.[64]

Following the wave of Black Lives Matter protests that erupted around the world and across Britain in the summer of 2020, including inspiring scenes of statues of slave traders tossed into the sea, lawmakers moved to crack down on the right to protest. These pushes to dampen public resistance to oppression were codified in the 2023 Police, Crime, Sentencing and Courts Act, despite fierce resistance from 'Kill the Bill' protestors and acts of civil disobedience sparked by police assaulting mourners at the Sisters Uncut vigil following Sarah Everard's death. The same Act sought to criminalise Gypsy, Roma and Traveller communities. We have also seen an uptick in show trial–style prosecutions of grass-roots organisers, showing that the judiciary are primed to punish anyone who dares make demands for social change that challenges state power. This was made clear in the trials of the Stansted Fifteen, who took peaceful action to stop a deportation charter flight in 2017, and the Colston Four, who were accused of 'damaging' the statue of slave trader Edward Colston. In this pressurised context, organising while surviving, and *in order* to survive, requires exploring all possible methods for loosening and buckling the bars that cage us in a system of racial capitalism. This means expanding our movements to ensure that they are broad-based and strong, and pulling together all the resources at our disposal. This requires working with abundance of spirit in a context of intense scarcity, anticipating the potential discovery of comrades everywhere we turn. While carceral feminism blunders on, creating more and more laws in pursuit of a dystopian vision of safety that seems to include incarcerating as many classed and racialised men as possible, there are rays of hope emerging. While still an embryonic current next to the monolith of the state-aligned carceral 'women's sector', abolitionist feminists – those who seek to prevent harm rather than simply punish it, and who see police, prisons and borders as powerful perpetrators of violence – are growing in number and confidence. The feminist divide is by no means generational. While social movements posing radical and abolitionist demands are commonly youth-led, many feminist organisers who bring wisdom from the preceding decades have continued to reject carceral feminism and its attendant chorus of racism, transphobia, Islamophobia and anti–sex work attitudes, instead providing critical and invaluable steers to our struggles. Writing in 2020 for OpenDemocracy, Amrit Wilson, a co-founder of AWAZ in the 1970s, writes, 'Abolition feminism points us to a horizon. To move towards it we must try and imagine a world without the oppressive carceral structures we have grown used to.'

A horizon is a tantalising point in the distance. Whether launching campaigns in the 1970s to challenge 'virginity' testing at Heathrow, or protesting the incarceration of women in detention centres in the 2010s, those seeking liberation journey towards that horizon as it remains eternally out of reach. This shifting dance towards futures of radical care is the praxis of abolition. Knowing that we may never touch the horizon, we can sculpt a forwards trajectory that is a living, breathing example of all that we might dream to discover, at that point where the land meets the sky.

5

Defund, Abolish, Now

Harm is a collective problem (with collective consequences) and there-fore requires collective solutions.

Sarah Lamble

What if abolition is something that grows?

Alexis Pauline Gumbs

Police abolition as abundance, not absence

The police do not protect us. In fact, they actively mete out violence and uphold inequality. This has been the case since the inception of the police force. Every pound spent on policing, prisons, borders and all of their attendant bureaucracies is a pound that is not being spent on life-giving resources. Working from this position, we must now instead ask the question, 'What does it mean to build a world where we will be safe for the first time?' To paraphrase cultural critic and author Hari Ziyad, who writes in relation to dismantling prisons, police abolition is not about just closing down the institution of the police; it is about closing the chapter of history that birthed policing because it relies on violence to exist.[1]

Pushes to defund and abolish the police are sometimes framed as being 'American' demands, and it is suggested that the British police could not be defunded because its structure and funding model are too complex.[2] The two countries are, of course, differently constituted, and the UK's state funding structures are certainly intentionally opaque. The UK has one of the most expensive police institutions in the world. Most of the funding for this costly 'service' comes from the Home Office, and about a third of funds are raised through Council Tax payments.[3] Since the mid-2010s, the spending of policing budgets (and the ability to dismiss chief constables) has been controlled by metro mayors and police and crime commissioners (PCCs), replacing police authorities. Both of these positions are elected by the eligible voting public every four years. However, the role of PCCs has been hotly debated, with a Labour Party report published in the early years of the PCC structure dismissing the role as 'the spectre of an experiment that is failing'.[4] The 'democratic' nature of PCCs is also contested, given that PCCs largely come from ex-policing or legal backgrounds,[5] and the first PCC elections (which, like all elections, are held at sizeable cost) represented the 'lowest recorded level of participation at a peacetime non-local government election in the UK'.[6] Accusations of cronyism among PCCs have been rife, alongside suggestions that crime budget spending is skewed by PCCs who are focused on their own re-election, for example through allocating more police officers to areas where the PCCs' support base lives.[7] A recent House of Lords debate also noted that police officers facing serious misconduct proceedings had been appointed to senior posts in PCC offices, and that mechanisms for holding PCCs to account were limited by budget restraints.[8]

In the early 2000s, police budgets were sizeable and the number of police officers grew rapidly, until cuts were announced in 2010 along with other public sector budget restrictions.[9] This didn't lead policing to shrink. Forces were instead encouraged to engage in partnerships with the private sector, including companies such as G4S, and other forms of state policing such as Border Force, MI5 and MI6. Specialist firearms officers and National Crime Agency officers also increased in number.[10] Funds removed from police budgets by the government were not diverted towards supporting life-affirming institutions that would reduce harm in society – the police were not 'defunded'. This budget reduction arrived in step with heavy privatisation efforts, wider securitisation across state agencies, and swingeing public funding cuts across the board that pushed people into poverty and entrenched physical and mental ill health. At the same time, the remit of police forces was expanded.

Police funding started steadily rising again towards the end of the 2010s, and in 2019 the government pledged to bring an additional 20,000 officers into the force via the Police Uplift Programme, at a potential cost of £500 million in the first year of recruitment.[11] In 2023, £17 billion was allocated to police in England and Wales, marking a rise of around 40 per cent in police funding since 2016.[12] Starting to 'defund' the institution of the police, in relatively simple terms, could have looked like immediately channelling the estimated additional £500 million earmarked for police recruitment in 2019 into healthcare services, economic assistance, social housing and community-based support and welfare (while also recognising the need for overhaul and longer-term replacement of these institutions), alongside dramatically restricting the role of police. Instead, the government opted to expand police powers. This also ramped up during the COVID-19 pandemic, a period in which huge numbers of people were pushed into poverty and lost their lives due to chronically underfunded health services, inadequate housing and a persistent crisis of harm in society undergirded by structural inequality and over a decade of austerity.

The carceral feminist triad: rape, child abuse and murder

Police abolition can be an incredibly difficult idea to grapple with because it can activate personal experiences of trauma, and therefore we must be guided by the experiences of survivors of all forms of violence, including state violence. Those of us who advocate police abolition, many of us survivors, are understandably often asked to explain what we would 'do' with people whose actions might be considered objectively abhorrent: the rapists, the child abusers and the murderers. These forms of violence make up what I call the 'carceral feminist triad': three manifestations of abuse that are generally considered to be unacceptable in society, and that instil so much fear and pain that the mere suggestion of (what is sometimes imagined to be) *further* exposure to these types of violence can provoke strong responses. I codify the carceral feminist triad not by any means to suggest that these forms are indeed the 'worst' or most prevalent in a hierarchy of violence. In fact, the triad invisibilises widespread, coexistent and similarly fatal forms of racial and economic violence that also affect marginalised communities, such as poverty and environmental degradation. The carceral feminist triad instead points towards how the carceral system taps into collectively held and deeply emotional responses to these topics in particular, which are further amplified by the way in which these types of violence are sensationally and gratuitously represented in media and popular culture. It also acts as a cognitive 'gotcha' that is levied against those who advocate police abolition, suggesting that defunding and abolition are not viable given the unique threat that the carceral feminist triad of violence poses.

The struggle for police abolition is steered by work to reduce all forms of violence and harm in society. Due to the strength and sincerity of this commitment, the mere illusion of safety and protection is not good enough. Abolition pushes us to address the root causes of harm while also rejecting structures and systems that do not actually benefit communities, and that in fact inflict further harm on the overwhelming majority of us. When those of us advocating abolition are asked what we would 'do' about the carceral feminist triad if police no longer existed, abolitionist Angel Parker provides a useful response to encourage this conversation forwards: 'what are we doing with them now?'[13] Right now, the police do not prevent rape. Even when rape is reported after the fact, only 1–2 per cent of rapes are prosecuted. This means that the promise of reporting rape as a way to prevent further harm to other people is not fulfilled by the police. Equally, right now, the police do not prevent murder, and nonetheless violent 'crime' has actually reduced by two-thirds since 1995 (a detail often obscured by statistics that show increased police recordings of 'violent crime' despite an overall much lower incidence).[14]

We know that policing tactics such as stop and search, raids and the gangs matrix do not prevent murder, rape and child abuse, and that police interventions in domestic violence situations often do not stop murders from happening. On this latter point, since 2011, statutory domestic homicide reviews (DHRs) have been carried out after any murder of a person aged over sixteen by an intimate partner, relative or household member. Analysis of DHRs gives us an indication of the demographics of people for whom the police fail to intervene and prevent murder in a domestic abuse context: recent data showed that the majority of victims (61 per cent) were vulnerabilised by a lack of support around alcohol and drug use, and also experienced mental health problems. Some 71 per cent of people who had murdered someone also experienced problems with alcohol and drug use as well as poor mental health. Some 60 per cent had a 'previous offending history' and 52 per cent were known to the police, indicating that prior criminal-legal interventions and contact with police had been ineffective in preventing the murder they later carried out.[15] It's evident that police do not prevent murder, and that even when people become known to the police for prior violent acts, in many cases police responses are not successful in preventing further, fatal forms of violence.

Another justification posed for carceral responses to the carceral feminist triad is the contested idea that people who carry out repeated acts of manipulation and extreme violence that are accompanied by a lack of empathy or remorse, some of whom are diagnosed as having antisocial personality disorders (such as what was previously referred to in medical and legal settings as 'psychopathy'), are understood as being immune to rehabilitation.[16] From this position, the carceral logic follows that the only viable response to people diagnosed as having antisocial personality disorders (ASPD) who also perform violent acts of lawbreaking outside state agendas is policing and prisons.

The pathologisation of behaviours that are grouped together in an ASPD diagnosis is heavily contested, and the existence of diagnostic frameworks does not constitute a fixed and immutable 'knowing' of a complex range of human experiences. As Micha Frazer-Carroll, author of *Mad World*, explained to me, 'Our concepts of "illness" and "disorder" are not God-given categories – they are shaped by the social, political and economic expectations of our society. The concept of the "psychopath" or the "antisocial personality", in particular, is a deeply political one, which often leads to very violent outcomes for people who receive this diagnosis.'

The clinicalisation of violent behaviours and responses to trauma in particular is in many cases used to support a carceral response for people with ASPD diagnoses. As Micha continues, 'Antisocial personality disorder sits at the intersection of medicalisation and criminalisation: the concept of psychopathy is used to bolster the inevitability of the criminal justice system, and reifies this idea that there are people who are inherently criminal and always will be, and aren't viable candidates for rehabilitation/recovery. Even the DSM makes reference to "criminal behaviour", which is obviously a very social and moral judgment, masquerading as an objective one.'

The diagnostic framework for ASPD is used to intensify carceral responses to certain forms of violence that are deemed potentially disruptive to the status quo, but not ones that prop up racial capitalism and imperial interests – as the Marxist legal blogger Habeas Quaestus notes: 'Arguably, many of the worst killers of the world did not even have personality disorders if we include every military general, every company that stoked conflict to make profits, and other socially sanctioned forms of mass murder.'[17]

We should continue to question the idea that any group of people who have caused harm (and in the case of people diagnosed with ASPDs, are statistically likely themselves to have been harmed) could be unresponsive to rehabilitation. Much more work, and much more resourcing for and learning from and within ASPD and mental health communities, are needed to understand the support needs of people experiencing mental distress and exhibiting a range of behaviours that may be harmful to themselves and others; as Micha explained to me, 'An important alternative to police in these situations is actually prevention.' The idea of mental ill health and distress as an experience or state that affects a discrete, fixed and nominal group of people should also be refuted. Given that ASPDs are diagnosed at a rate of three in a hundred people,[18] irrespective of our mental health in the present moment and whether we accept or reject such pathologisations, we would be prescient to eliminate violent systems and institutions that many have already been subjected to, knowing that all of us could come into contact with them at any time (to different degrees of risk), with or without our consent, as the mental health of all of us fluctuates over the course of our lives.

Outside the pathologisation of violence, the web of factors that contribute to the incredibly small number of people who perform repeated acts of extreme violence and cruelty is complex and shifting. Continued exploration of this is the work of people with a range of healing and community-based expertise, and not police officers and agents of the state. It is hard to quantify how many people in the UK perform acts of extreme violence (and again, 'extreme' by whose measure?), and for whom some degree of at least temporary separation from community might be necessary for public safety. In order to get a sense of this landscape we might consider that only sixty-six people are currently in prison on whole-life orders, meaning that they will spend the rest of their life in prison due to the extremity of their violent acts.[19] We can surmise that many more people continue to act with impunity, and that despite the existence of the carceral system, wealth and power are likely to prevent many of these people from facing any kind of accountability. This tells us that with or without the current (non-functioning) carceral system, there is a relatively small group of people who are deemed to be unquestionably harmful to society, within current legal and medical frameworks. Equally, many of the other extreme forms of violence that currently don't fall into the purview of the criminal-legal system would not increase as a result of police abolition – and in fact an abolitionist approach would place emphasis on reducing harm both caused and experienced by this much wider category of people.

The process of reporting rape or child abuse and seeking a prosecution is incredibly re-traumatising for survivors, and the majority of withdrawal from cases happens at the pre-charge phases, when survivors are engaging with police.[20] A recent review of rape investigations also evidenced that police fail to meet basic access needs such as sign language interpreters for deaf survivors.[21] Even if a prosecution is somehow obtained, prisons do not reduce harm: in the minute number of cases where people serve custodial sentences for acts of rape, they are locked up in prisons which are themselves sites of sexual violence – reports of which have skyrocketed in the past decade.[22] This sort of 'eye for an eye' response may offer temporary psychic relief to the survivor, but fundamentally does little to prevent that person from harming again in future.

Instead, policies of criminal punishment and laws relating to sexual violence, murder and child abuse are often shaped and skewed around high-profile cases and the subsequent media discourse and public opinion which unfold in their aftermath. For example, in the wake of the murder of two-year-old James Bulger by two ten-year-old boys in 1993, politicians of all stripes called for a 'tough on crime' approach, with then shadow home secretary Tony Blair giving a strident speech about the 'moral chaos' that befalls a society that fails to 'teach the value of what is right and what is wrong'.[23] The law and order approach that Blair would implement throughout his prime ministership sought to court public outrage sparked by a handful of abominable murder cases, which did not by any means represent the general demographic of people who would be subjected to these ever-more draconian carceral policies. By eschewing an evidence-based or harm reduction approach, police and criminal responses to the carceral feminist triad fail to make society 'safer', instead raining down punishment after abuse has occurred.

Where concerns around child abuse fall under the joint remit of police and social services, child protection proceedings can often present punitive, classed, racialised and bordered responses to issues of poverty, with state funds channelled into separation procedures that could instead be used to support families' material needs. US-based scholar Dorothy Roberts calls this ever-lurking threat of children being taken away the 'family policing system'. An amplified culture of 'safeguarding' has sprung up around statutory bodies' anxiety about allegations of ineptitude, while the confected association between marginalised children and higher levels of 'risk' enables policing by the backdoor. In many cases, statutory responses to children are themselves the site of abuse, violence and neglect. For example, in the case of children going through the asylum system, age assessment 'tests' that are devoid of any scientific basis are used to block children from accessing support and welfare services. Likewise, cultures of contempt within local authority social services mean that service provision is often poor or absent even when a child is deemed eligible for support. In a recent case, seventy-six asylum-seeking children went missing from a Home Office hostel in Brighton where local social workers were supposed to be working with families, leading a Conservative MP to shout in Parliament that 'they shouldn't have come here illegally'.[24]

Many survivors' experiences of abuse are horrific, life-changing and acutely painful in ways that endure and chip away at us; at the same time there are ways in which our experiences can transform us beyond roles of victimhood. The criminal-legal system is not invested in this transformation: one in which we utilise our expertise as survivors to reduce harm and build new worlds, and also in which we are not socially abandoned if we cause harm, despite the fact that through our abusive acts we may have sought to deny the humanity of others. This system is not set up to lead us down a path of healing and justice in all the forms that matter to us, and it doesn't encourage people to apologise and account for what they have done. As attorney Cassandra Mensah explains, writing for *Teen Vogue*, 'Perpetrators cannot admit to wrongdoing without confessing to a crime and so have no incentive to do so.'[25]

People who are wealthy and powerful whose actions sit in the crosshairs of the carceral feminist triad on the whole evade criminal-legal consequences, and manage to harm multiple people over long stretches of time. Even when there is common knowledge that someone is explicitly and serially abusive, professional and class status can enable them to act abusively with impunity, despite the fact that police are allegedly 'keeping us safe'. Instead, the delivery of 'criminal justice' largely works to maintain structural inequality in society. What does it mean that people are more likely to be incarcerated who are working-class; Black; Muslim; disabled; experiencing mental illness; sex workers; survivors of violence themselves in huge numbers; care leavers; members of Gypsy, Roma and Traveller communities; or neurodiverse? This situation does not deliver 'justice', by any stretch of the word.

Towards community safety

The fact that police are not currently keeping us safe or preventing violence provides us with the basis for police abolition. We need the means to survive and thrive in order to approach any form of safety and freedom from harm. The range of services, networks and infrastructure that communities need (and are best placed to design and build) is better detailed elsewhere, but we all urgently need access to safe and comfortable housing; nutritious food; mutual aid and networks of care; rest and recuperation; patient-centred healthcare and healing; access to carefully stewarded green space; active, intellectual and creative fulfilment, and more. Rather than pursuing more and more ways to put more people into cages, feminists looking to sculpt a world of care and compassion might pour their energies into organising around safe and affordable housing, and participate in efforts to more widely distribute essential resources through community kitchens and gardens and other mutual aid and well-being projects, or any number of life-giving, community-building activities. After all, when feminists began to organise around domestic violence and rape, they did not build makeshift prisons. They found physical spaces for women to find safety and community, and they worked to take care of each other.

In addition to securing the means to thrive, it's important to consider what types of community-based harm reduction programmes and systems we can call on and develop in the immediate term to prevent and reduce harms that people experience and indeed cause, even in contexts where they have most of their needs met. In a resource on police abolition written by Jared Knowles and Andrea J. Ritchie, the authors advocate for the use of 'violence interruptors' in the form of 'respected community members' – instead of police – who carry out daily community outreach in order to 'de-escalate, prevent and intervene in potentially violent situations', as well as following up if harm is caused in order to stop escalation and retaliation.[26] This method has been used in Baltimore in the US, where in 2021 a Safe Streets programme marked one year without any homicides in one of their areas.[27] UK-based academic Guy Aitchison also proposes alternatives to the police in the form of a permanent body staffed by members of the community on rotation, much like the way jury duty currently operates. The rotation of staff both could prevent the hoarding of power by a few individuals, and might work to disperse institutional interest in expanding their powers, weaponry and resources.[28] This system would also disseminate skills such as de-escalation and conflict resolution throughout communities.

A number of community-based harm reduction and harm prevention methods and approaches already exist, building on informal tactics that marginalised communities have used for centuries, given that the police have never had our backs. In my conversation with a grass-roots organiser, they talked me through different ways in which communities are building skills to prevent harm. This includes interventions and strategies at different levels, such as doing deep relational work with our loved ones so that we can have conversations about violence and look out for each other, learning about what harassment or sexual violence looks like and how to prevent and support harm within our communities, and sharing resources such as spare rooms, emergency funds and childcare support, which can all be used to relieve the stressors that can cause harm to escalate without resorting to calling the police.

Not calling the police also looks like abandoning abstract moralising and switching on our common sense to try and figure out why harm is happening and what the root causes might be. I was recently in a large chain supermarket when a woman who tried to leave without paying for a bag of items was apprehended aggressively by security guards who threatened to call the police. Multiple members of the public stepped in to stop the violence and assist the woman in getting away, stating that there is a cost-of-living crisis and people need food. Due to the intervention, the woman was able to take her food and leave without further harm; the huge profit-making supermarket would have barely registered a few missing groceries.

Similarly, bystander intervention programmes run by groups and organisations such as Hollaback in the late 2010s, and currently Level Up, Cradle Community and Remember & Resist, among others, equip us with skills to support people who are experiencing harassment in public spaces (including by state actors). Bystander intervention seeks to centre the needs and wishes of the person being harassed, often with a view to quickly shutting down the abuse and eliminating the need to call the police. Interventions also have the impact of indicating to the person causing harm that their behaviour is not acceptable and will not be tolerated and enabled, without escalating the situation. In a more connected community working on the basis of transformative justice, a bystander takes note of the person causing harm as someone who needs support or attention, and takes appropriate steps to ensure this is followed up, with a view to preventing further incidents.

This work provides a viable alternative to pouring energy into 'holding police to account' and criticising them for 'failing to act', given that marginalised communities know that police action itself is a threat to life. Janey spoke to me about her experience running bystander intervention workshops with the feminist organisation Level Up, and noted a particular way in which white feminist busybodies can put their 'skills' to use: '[There is] this very specific demographic of women in their sixties called Elaine who were really keen! And it's the first time I've witnessed the power of the Karen for good. Because they really were taking notes on like, "OK that's PACE [the Police and Criminal Evidence Act 1984]. And is it under sixteen or seventeen where there has to be an appropriate adult?" ... I cannot tell you in my organising lifetime where I've seen that specific demographic involved in wanting to challenge the police and I do think something has shifted and we have to keep pulling that needle.'

This type of action may feel clunky or strange at first, as the successful elevation of the police as the 'only solution' to harm has psychologically stripped us of our own powers to act. The only way out of this bind is to practise and normalise intervening with care and compassion – as a community organiser reminded me, 'It's like a muscle we have to develop, to step into dealing with stuff, because we've been taught to step back.'

⤳

When children experience abuse, including sexual abuse, it is overwhelmingly from people inside their own households, and not from strangers. Implicit denial of this through the production and consumption (in popular culture, in the education system, in mainstream media and in public policy) of 'stranger danger' narratives glosses over the fact that the people we love harm us and also harm our loved ones. The idea that police are needed to hunt down the bogeymen 'out there' is propped up by a narrative that people who abuse children are not 'in here', sat on our sofas and around our dinner tables. This is a painful and concerning reality to engage with: recognising the prevalence of child abuse can make the task of harm reduction feel utterly overwhelming. Nonetheless, we need to operate on the basis of this reality. The Bay Area Transformative Justice Collective (BATJC) in Oakland in the US, for example, uses a 'pod-mapping' process to help us precisely articulate people within our communities who can support us with safety, accountability, healing and transformation of behaviours whether we turn for help as survivors, witnesses and bystanders, or as people who have harmed others.[29]

The terminology of 'pod-mapping' recognises that harm comes most commonly from within our communities and so it is insufficient to imagine or romanticise 'community' as a place of connectivity and safety for everyone at all times. BATJC has created a pod-mapping worksheet which invites us to specify the people who can support us (and receive our support), as well as identify people with whom we could build more trust and connection in order to bring them into our circle. As organiser Mia Mingus explained to Aviva Stahl for *Bustle*, pods create a clear network through which child abuse can be interrupted, meaning that we are positioned to have conversations with our community members if we see them, or become aware of them, mistreating a child in any way.[30]

The structure of the 'family' itself poses a number of barriers to harm reduction, as Sophie Lewis explains in their book *Abolish the Family*. Lewis describes how families, in reality, are a 'harsh lottery' where care is privatised and devalued, and difficult dynamics – some abusive – are often shielded from outside interventions.[31] We must also chip away at the denial surrounding the way in which broader social norms (and our complicity in them) enable child abuse. Supporting children to have agency over their own bodies – for example by not forcing them to hug or kiss people, providing alternatives to hugs and kisses such as high fives or waving, and seeking consent when appropriate before touching – helps to develop a culture where children know that their bodies belong to them. This is by no means to suggest that the onus is on children to identify and set their bodily boundaries – it is certainly not – but it is to recognise that eliminating coercive forms of touching where possible reduces tactics that can be exploited and used to abuse and harm. In this context, the concept of 'safeguarding', then, must also be reconfigured. A radical safeguarding workbook written by Latifa Akay and Alex Johnston for the organisation Maslaha suggests that a child's 'best interests' might involve building anti-oppressive cultures in schools (and other institutions that children engage with) that strengthen young people's capacity and agency to consent and draw boundaries, and that enable all members of the respective institution to name harm and hold each other accountable.

It should be noted that body language and nonverbal communication look different within communities and across the world – touch, including of particular body parts, in one

geographical location or context may be considered very intimate but the same touch will be deemed quotidian in others.
However, it is important to be guided by the primacy of a child's
autonomy, and a child's preference, irrespective of whether
refusing or objecting to physical contact will be considered
'rude'.[32] Children from racialised groups and Black children
in particular face a compounded risk of having their bodily
autonomy violated by public and state actors due to the tendency
for Black children to be perceived as older or more 'mature' than
they are, and racist perceptions of their assumed strength (and
therefore potential to resist), as well as assumptions of pathological criminality. This was particularly evident in the strip-search
by police of a child – referred to as 'Child Q' – in a school in east
London in 2020. The violence, trauma and coercive terror of
police strip-searches, including of children, are normalised and
shielded by the state from the label of 'sexual violence' because
of the presumed consent of those who are searched. This is con-
tradicted by the fact that consent for a bodily violation enacted
by police is a questionable concept, as Koshka explained to me:
'If you comply with a sexual "request", or a sexualised request,
when there isn't the possibility of saying no, then that is already
a violent situation.'

It is essential to recognise the autonomy of children in order
to reduce harm, and in order not to lean into assumptions of
children being naive or inherently powerless, while also not
adultifying them along racialised lines. One survivor of grooming that I spoke with explained that disempowering depictions of
child abuse survivors in informational videos about child abuse
that she had watched at school prevented her from disclosing her
experiences to adults around her, noting, 'I'm a clever person,
and I felt like I'd fallen for something that people wouldn't

expect me to have fallen for. So then I feel that if I told anyone, they'd be like, "Oh, you're not as clever as I think you are" ... [informational videos about grooming] always portray the girls as like, "Oh, they don't know any better." And like, they're so innocent, and they don't know anything.'

Police and prisons do not present a viable solution to child abuse, given that they are not set up to prevent harm, and given that the power dynamic between adults and children obscures a vast amount of abuse that is perpetrated, typically by people who are within a child's immediate support network. One grooming survivor I spoke with acknowledged that while in the aftermath of an incident she wanted vengeance – 'I wanted to be like, send them away. Make them feel tiny. Like they've made me feel' – with some distance and reflection, she felt that education programmes and therapeutic interventions would make her feel safest. The recognition of this need for space and reflection before acting is crucial: Richie Reseda, a US-based abolitionist organiser, emphasises the need to make room for feelings of anger when we are harmed. Reseda encourages us to listen attentively to each other's fears and desires for revenge in order that we *don't* act on them. He writes, 'Deeply listening to oppressed ppl's anger is one of the most abolitionist things we can do.'[33]

For some survivors, the person abusing them may themselves be a police officer. We know that police officers are statistically likely to keep their jobs in law enforcement despite allegations of abuse;[34] this issue is so widespread that it was the subject of a super-complaint against the police in 2020, which reported that police were using their power and status to quash allegations made against them.[35] Given that the police have proved to be a source of violence for many of us, and also to their own families, survivors have for a long time developed strategies to keep safe without police contact. Safety plans can include packing an emergency bag which contains important things a person might need if they had to leave home in a hurry, such as important documents and cash, as well as co-ordinating signals with neighbours to indicate that they need help, such as turning particular lights on or off, or placing a particular item in view on a windowsill.

During research in the western Balkans and Turkey in 2017 alongside the activist and academic Neha Kagal, I met with a range of women's organisations supporting marginalised survivors of violence (including Roma, Egyptian and Ashkali women; disabled women; LGBTQI people; and women living in rural areas), who explained that survivors have 'a thousand ways to solve our problems' without engaging with the police or the criminal-legal system. Instead of pushing for police reporting, these groups used community-based safety strategies such as hosting drop-in sessions where women could leave the family home and socialise, relax and heal, and opening their homes to each other if survivors intuited that it would be safer to be away from their family home for a period of time.[36] Kagal's research as a member of a waste picker's union in India also indicated that union membership itself was a strategy through which women were able to reduce the harm of domestic violence. Through what union members described as an emboldened sense of self and entitlement to be in the marital home due to their material contributions to it, survivors transferred the skills they learnt in the union space into the domestic space, shifting from tactics of bargaining to making demands backed up by the threat of withdrawing their labour and earnings.[37]

Another crucial strategy for preventing and addressing inter-personal violence in relationships and families is to develop a culture of openness and accountability in how we relate to each other. Janey explains that a primary step to reducing violence involves 'putting a culture of honesty around our intimate partner relationships, and all of us talking to each other about what's going on and modelling that ... there is this myth that what happens in private is that couple's business and nobody else's – its only ever after the fact when something goes really wrong that someone is like "oh I never liked him anyway".'

For Janey, this culture of honesty also extends to compassion-ately checking each other if we are speaking disrespectfully about our partners and loved ones, even in their absence. Becoming well versed in the key indicators of domestic abuse and coercive control is a way in which we can look out for those around us, and help each other to spot the warning signs of relationships that are, or could become, harmful.

Anti-police responses to the carceral feminist triad that hold harm reduction as a guiding principle include processes of community accountability and transformative justice (TJ). TJ provides a way to respond to situations of harm outside state institutions, with a particular emphasis on healing that is 'trans-formative', and on nurturing the contexts, tools and tactics for violence prevention along the way. TJ as a practice has long roots in many communities globally, as writer, educator and trainer Mia Mingus writes:

> Indigenous communities, black communities, immigrant com-munities ... poor and low-income communities, communities of color, people with disabilities, sex workers, queer and trans com-munities ... have been practicing TJ in big and small ways for

generations – trying to create safety and reduce harm within the dangerous conditions they were and are forced to live in.[38]

Common characteristics of TJ include what Mingus describes as building and using a combination of community infrastructure (e.g. safe houses, a network of conflict de-escalators), skills (conflict resolution, healing practices) and ways of relating (care and compassion) as a generative response and preventive approach to harm that doesn't involve calling the police. As Melanie Brazzell explains in *Abolishing the Police*, unlike policing, TJ practices are acutely tailored to the needs of communities. They write, 'This is the granular work of change, not a one-size-fits-all approach.'[39] Through recognising that violence is a product of social and economic conditions under racial capitalism (as a survivor of grooming told me, 'no one is born a rapist'), we can take collective responsibility for reducing harm. The 'purpose' of TJ is fluid and shifting depending on the needs of the situation; sometimes stopping the violence will be a primary concern, whereas in a case of a disclosure of historic abuse, an accountability process may take precedence. As a mode of TJ, community accountability (CA) was codified by INCITE! (a US-based network of feminists of colour), in recognition that preventing and responding to harm effectively requires community action. The tremendous vitality, scope and possibility of TJ and CA processes are explored in detail elsewhere, and we should be inspired and encouraged in our abolitionist struggles by the careful and tireless work of reimagining justice, for the benefit of all of us.

The revolution will not be state-funded

The charity-sectorisation or NGO-isation of feminist activity in the UK is by no means a unique phenomenon. The vast majority of small grass-roots groups have been forced to either close their doors, or to adapt, expand and formalise their work in order to sustain it. The accompanying 'professionalisation' is both pushed and pulled by available sources of funding – including from trusts and foundations, whose grants have outpaced economic growth over the past fifteen years. Trusts and foundations are also not immune to the fluctuations of the financial market, and in the early period of the COVID-19 pandemic, many experienced dips in the value of their investment portfolios, which had a knock-on impact on cash flow.[40] In spite of this, trust and foundation spending rose hugely in 2020, in part due to a wave of significant donations and the creation of new funds.

The other large source of funding for NGO-ised groups is the state, which increasingly engages small charities in public sector contracts. Yet there is no such thing as a free lunch and accepting state funding restricts organisations in what they can say and do, obliging them to effectively uphold the status quo or risk their funding being cut. State funding tacitly tasks feminist organisations with the work of reinforcing and validating state power and its various institutions and agendas. For example, Ministry of Justice-funded independent domestic violence advocates (IDVAs) and independent sexual violence advocates (ISVAs) heavily lean towards survivor engagement with the system of criminal punishment, while funding provided via the government's Islamophobic 'counterterrorism' laws for 'race equality' organisations, domestic violence support services and women's organisations is described by organisers as carrying a heavy surveillance emphasis.[41] A Home Office document leaked in 2015 revealed how Prevent-funded Muslim community groups were being explicitly used to bolster state agendas, for example in order to 'undermine the extremist narrative that we are at war with Islam', and to 'encourage British Muslim women to make a stand and take the lead to reject ISIL propaganda',[42] providing yet more evidence for the instrumentalisation of Muslim women in the service of British imperial interests.[43]

Trusts and foundations similarly have their own agendas and particular interests, which community organisations and charities must bend towards in order to secure financial support. While trusts and foundations may be well intentioned, funding is often 'project-based' (e.g. intended to support a defined, measurable, short term-project, often with emphasis on 'innovation' and conditional on tangible outcomes) as opposed to supporting longer-term work or core costs. As Paula X. Rojas writes in *The Revolution Will Not Be Funded*,

> Foundation funders and the non-profit culture expect groups to achieve a campaign goal in a relatively short period of time. They are not interested in funding the much slower work of base building, which takes years and years to do. Consequently, non-profits become short-term goal oriented ... Many also become focused on 'smoke and mirrors' organizing, in which you do something that looks good for a photo op but has no real people power behind it.[44]

The common outcome of receiving state funding, and to a slightly lesser degree trust and foundation funding, is 'mission drift' – that groups get dragged into doing work that doesn't support their stated objectives, and that in fact may proactively hinder their own mission and demands. Ruth Wilson Gilmore, writing about her concerns with the anti-prison movement in the US, outlines the logical fallacy of aligning with the right wing (in our case in the form of state interests), 'as though a superficial overlap in viewpoint meant a unified structural analysis for action'.[45] The intertwining of mainstream feminism's desire for violence to be 'taken seriously' by the criminal-legal system, with the state's vested interest in criminalising (but not reducing) acts of violence, is a crude elision. The doubling down on carceral feminism which locates feminist solutions in the criminal-legal system represents a consistent tactic which believes that the 'mission' of liberation and justice will be achieved by criminal-legal means.

The NGO-isation of resistance also coerces organisers into uneasy alliances with the state and its agents via the permutations of the property market. For some of us it's hard to imagine that in the era of the GLC, some feminist organisations constructed or owned buildings, such as the purpose-built Jagonari Centre in Whitechapel; Al-Hasaniya Moroccan Women's Centre in Trellick Tower; Hungerford House, which was home to the precursor of the Feminist Library, and Tindlemanor among others. Increasing rental costs have increased the outgoings of groups and organisations who choose or need to operate from a physical premises; this pushes organisations into more professionalised charity structures in order to secure larger amounts of funding. In the present day, the implanting of charities into multipurpose buildings that are surveilled and privately securitised further embeds these organisations in the pluralised web of policing. These buildings are assets of racial capitalism, their 'safety' protected by guards who restrict entry to those who can swipe in and out while upholding structures of inequality. At the same time, when NGO-isation is resisted and groups have to gather in spaces that are not fit for purpose – when buildings are inaccessible and located far from transport hubs, are poorly lit or heated, and are poorly designed or too small, preventing essential parallel services such as creches and breakout or well-being spaces – organising is restricted to those who can pass through these barriers unhindered.

The route out of the conditions that accompany state funding or grants from trusts and foundations is unlikely to involve demanding more funding from those same sources to support radical work. I spoke with a charity sector funding specialist who explained that seeking funding from trusts and foundations, or the corporate social responsibility arms of businesses that are elsewhere perpetuating inequality, does not bring us closer to liberation. They noted that 'foundations are putting around 96 per cent of their money into things that are causing the problem a lot of the time and then [only] 4 per cent which goes to charity … it's gonna forever be a cycle, it doesn't really matter if they give unrestricted grants if they're still investing in things that are killing PoC, queer people and trans people'. In the immediate term, Paula X. Rojas explains that there is space for more radical groups to harness the resources of existing NGOs (such as technical support, tools and skills), without those same NGOs determining the direction of the wider social movement.[46]

NGOs might dissolve once they have suitably disseminated skills. Or perhaps NGOs or charities are set up as public-facing 'fronts' while grass-roots groups self-organise their membership; the NGO doesn't hold any information on members or decision-making power over the membership, so that it doesn't collapse if funding is lost.[47] In the meantime, there is perhaps potential for larger charities to operate effectively alongside radical grass-roots groups. Lucy McKay from INQUEST described to me how there is a place for both activism and policy organisations, as they explain: 'You need [an organisation] who has their foot in the door to actually influence and make the changes, and maybe they make compromises and you don't always get it, right. But you also need the people on the outside who are shouting loudly for much more fundamental stuff, and are shifting the culture and shifting public understanding towards the bigger picture.'

By moving away from traditional funding relationships, over the past few years many groups and informal collectives have shown that crowdfunding and raising money through small (and sometimes regular) donations from large numbers of people, or through a subscription membership model as used by trade unions, can be very effective. This is by no means a contemporary invention, as mutual aid in the UK has deep roots in Black communities who set up self-help groups, rent parties and 'pardners' (independent savings collectives) in the late 1940s and the 1950s. Twenty-first-century iterations of community fundraising have proved fruitful: Black Lives Matter UK (UKBLM) received £1.2 million in donations to its online crowdfunder in the summer of 2020, which saw widespread protests across the UK in the wake of the murder of George Floyd in Minneapolis, in the context of a long history of anti-racist struggle on British soil. After proceeding through a robust grant-making process, UKBLM has since disseminated over half of these funds to anti-racist and abolitionist groups, including police monitoring organisations, LGBTQ support groups and health organisations run by and for Black communities.

Many groups and organisations set up 'hardship funds' during the COVID-19 pandemic, similarly demonstrating potential ways of collecting funds without being entangled in state policies or the agendas of trusts and foundations. The Sex Worker

Advocacy and Resistance Movement (SWARM) gave out £251,000 in grants to 1,255 sex workers in 2020 through their hardship fund. SWARM have subsequently produced a resource on how to run a mutual aid fund, which includes information on operational logistics and administration (such as data collection and verifying applicants), and reflections on the positive outcomes and challenges, including police diverting sex workers to reapply to SWARM's hardship fund in order to try and move them on.[48]

When organising groups are funded by and therefore directly accountable to our communities, space opens up to imagine solutions that dream beyond the narrow confines of state agencies such as the police. Groups and organisations working in this way push beyond the confines of charity status, reports for funders and navigating the Gothic halls of parliamentary lobbying. This may prove unappealing for some individuals who have attained a degree of financial security and social and cultural capital through their 'careers' working on issues such as gender-based violence. During our conversation, a worker from the GBV sector posed a useful question: 'We have seen many women who've gained by embracing these types of [professionalised] systems. And so how do we separate ourselves from a system where actually for some women, it reaps great benefit?'

Detaching from sources of funding that necessarily upholds the status quo surfaces important questions around workers' livelihoods and the sustainability and scalability of their work without reliable funding. For this reason, Paula X. Rojas's writings on the ways in which NGOs can submit themselves to being harnessed by grass-roots movements is particularly applicable to a UK context: what would it mean for large, well-funded feminist charities to make themselves indispensable to, not extractive of, abolitionist movements that are lead by marginalised people experiencing the sharp edge of state violence? What would it mean for mainstream feminism to perform a critical audit of the way in which it hoards and utilises power and influence, and to meaningfully share its resources (funds, contacts, spaces, staff, technology, skills) widely with groups who want them, and who cannot access more formal funding pathways? Such a devolution would need to be led by the demands of marginalised feminist and abolitionist groups to ensure that larger NGOs did not simply absorb their expertise in order to bolster their own, persistently carceral, objectives. It is likely that many large, well-funded feminist organisations would not be willing to release their grip on their carceral and careerist motives, and such organisations are unlikely to prove useful allies in any struggle for a different world.

We have the opportunity to focus on redirecting resources towards life-giving institutions rather than the Sisyphean work of reforming an unreformable institution. This orientation frees up capacity for marginalised communities to set the agenda and lead on the work of defining what safety and justice really mean in practice. We must remember that the exact things that reformists wish to 'improve' about the police and the carceral system – that it is violent, that it targets marginalised communities, that it perpetuates cycles of harm and poverty, and that it fails, astronomically, to keep us all safe – are, as academic Marina Bell describes, 'intrinsic to the logic of how it is intended to work'.[49]

While law reforms may – for a minuscule cohort of people – facilitate the ability to lock up those who have harmed them, or may marginally ease the often retraumatising and largely dead-end process of reporting harm to the criminal-legal system, at the macro level the creation of new criminal offences leads to the targeting, punishment and social abandonment of marginalised groups without interrupting cycles of harm or preventing violence. When those who have committed harm are police officers themselves, 'accountability' processes via bodies such as the Independent Office for Police Conduct (IOPC) may offer symbolic forms of justice – which in a context of grinding oppression and barely existent recognition of the pain that state violence causes is of course a significant feat – but at the same time may falsely give the impression of atonement by a system that is premised upon violence and death.

Love as acts of freedom from police

During one period of writing this book, after weeks on end of late nights, infrequent meals and saturating myself with the pounding surf of violent information – in the form of testimonies, podcasts, books, social media disclosures, videos, interviews, academic journals, police reports, legal proceedings, archival material including pamphlets and newsletters, my own memories and those of my loved ones and ancestors, and a host of legislation printed on paper and carved in stone – I was swallowed whole. My research bled into my dreams. At night I imagined myself besieged by a host of violent actors – some tried to burn me alive in my house, others chased me across fields and high fences. In one dream in which I was locked in a remote shed and left to die, as a sadistic quirk of the narrative I helped my captors locate a metal grille that they would later secure to the doorway, before I realised their intentions. At the end of the dream my mind confected cinematic end titles which showed newspaper clippings explaining that my starved corpse had been discovered seven weeks later. By day, I had no appetite and I drifted hazily through the city, avoiding all thoughts of returning to writing.

Seeking to catch a breeze and shake off the dust, I took the Metro to the coast. I walked into the sea and let the cold waves steal my breath. I sank under the surface and felt myself fall back into my body. I gasped in the palm of the sea, and I exhaled then for all of us who could not breathe.[50] In the water, my molecules coexisted with those of grains of sand, small fish and tendrils of seaweed. I thanked my ancestors. A small wave splashed its salts onto my lips. It whispered of crisps, fries, soy sauce and all things curative. I swam back to shore, feeling the muscles in my legs fire up to kick against the gentle surf. I took some days away from my laptop, I ate, drank, inhaled deeply as I walked under orange trees; I masticated my struggle and digested it along with sips of decaf coffee and wine. These ancient grapes had refined the art of collective sustenance. I realised that I had failed to embody the lessons that dissenters, organisers, bodies of water and other organic matter across the centuries had been passing across time and space: it is only through caring for ourselves and each other that we can survive. This cannot be care for the self at the sacrifice of others (or vice versa), but these are what bell hooks describes as the acts of love that are necessary for liberation, or 'love as the practice of freedom'.[51]

Without a committed practice of care, the trauma of both living and working closely with violence (in its different forms and degrees) both erodes the potency of any work to end violence, and at the same time restricts the breathing space of life itself. The continued inclination for (some of) those doing feminist work to support and ally with the police is an indicator of the chipping away of the radical politics of collective care which provides daily nutrients for movements for change. Care, and therefore survival, is the primary act of resistance to the systematic enforcement of premature death. The movement for police abolition must sit squarely on foundations of care. Yet within the mainstream and NGO-ised feminist movement, the narrative has taken hold instead that police abolition is too utopian, and that our present realities are too fast-moving and dangerous, to consider abolition of the institutions that enforce violence (while offering protection for a limited few). Countering this tendency requires developing a daily devotion of radical love and care as a first port of call. This practice can and will take many forms.

Expanding the cosmos of the feminist imagination

A slogan graffitied on a wall in Paris during a period of widespread strikes and occupations of universities and factories in the summer of 1968 (known as 'May '68'), read, 'Un flic dort en chacun de nous, il faut le tuer' ('A cop sleeps inside every one of us; we must kill him'). Divesting from the carceral system does not just involve abolition of the police, but pushes us to examine how we absorb carceral logics into our daily decision making – the police officer in our head. Community organiser and academic Sarah Lamble describes this as a shift towards 'everyday abolition', a practice of not disposing of people who do or have done things that we don't like or that harm us.[52] Lamble gives examples of times when the police officer sleeping inside us awakens, such as when we moralise against lawbreaking as survival, like shoplifting in a supermarket, or when we demonstrate less interest or commitment to assisting someone get their basic needs met if they have previously harmed someone we care about. In order to expand our capacity for everyday abolition, many of us will need to upskill ourselves in conflict navigation and resolution. Leaning on practices of communication that organisers have been using for a long time, such as active listening, choosing to critique actions and ideas instead of individuals, and identifying and taking ownership for our feelings in order to clearly express what we need from others, enables us to better move through conflict between people who care for each other. Such an approach requires emotional vulnerability: expressing our desires and making requests which might be refused can feel precarious, but the alternative approach of silencing our needs keeps us at a distance from each other, and prevents us from building close and reliable bonds of community.

In *From Margin to Center*, bell hooks implores us to build new value systems and to actively reconceptualise power in ways that don't require the domination of others. In *Braiding Sweetgrass*, Robin Wall Kimmerer also explores indigenous knowledge forms and the teachings of plants, and offers the expression of gratitude as a revolutionary idea: 'In a consumer society, contentment is a radical proposition. Recognizing abundance rather than scarcity undermines an economy that thrives by creating unmet desires. Gratitude cultivates an ethic of fullness, but the economy needs emptiness.'[53]

Wall Kimmerer captures the incompatibility between a capitalist economy premised upon scarcity for the many (and wealth for the few), and ethics of 'abundance' which provide the fertile ground for abolition. Value systems are, of course, intimately linked to material conditions which define and are defined by shared social attitudes and priorities. Research suggests that women having autonomy and equality in decision making and resource distribution within families, as well as conceptualisations of masculinity being delinked from domination, are key components for situations of low violence.[54] The Marxist philosopher Antonio Gramsci describes this web of controlling forces as 'hegemony': a form of leadership that is simultaneously 'cultural, moral and ideological'.[55] The creation of a counterhegemony, according to Gramsci, involves exorcising this miasma of controlling ideas and conditions through active destabilisation of the status quo. This is enacted through the ways in which we live our lives; through how we build collective social and political power; through how we relate to each other as comrades, lovers, workers, carers, healers and community members; through how we relate to property, to the things we create and to the earth; and through how we learn and organise together.

Centuries of domination have resulted in a huge amount of violence and death, and so we must open up spaces to collectively grieve and express the pain of anti-violence and feminist work. The paucity of rituals in England surrounding grief and death, and the inadequacy of the English verbal and physical language to express mourning leave a limited site for sharing experiences of pain, loss and the potentially transformative dimension of grief. Gathering to express anger, to cry, to scream and to lament, do not fulfil performance indicators in NGO-ised feminist organisations. Reflecting on the need for spaces to express grief within Black social movements, hooks writes,

> Acknowledging the truth of our reality, both individual and collective, is a necessary stage for personal and political growth. This is usually the most painful stage in the process of learning to love – the one many of us seek to avoid ... Choosing love we also choose to live in community, and that means that we do not have to change by ourselves. We can count on critical affirmation and dialogue with comrades walking a similar path.[56]

hooks makes a critical point: that healing in community is assisted by the support of those around us who are struggling for the same freedoms. Ruth Wilson Gilmore writes that community-led abolition (of police, of prisons, of borders, of gender binaries, ostensibly of racism capitalism) is 'about presence, not absence. It's about building life-affirming institutions.'[57] Even the police themselves recognise the clear logic of abolition. Upon retirement, a Merseyside chief constable remarked, 'The best crime prevention is increased opportunity and reduced poverty,'[58] and advocated for diverting funds away from police and towards addressing destitution and unemployment. Healing for and through abolition is not about demolition, but about what we continue to build in the spaces where harm has been smoked out, and the ways in which we expand into those spaces. Abolition involves growing a web of ideas and experiments that have been trialled and tested; closing the gaps between these experiments and continually adapting and evolving our responses to violence so that they are as effective as possible.

The endless possibilities of abolition invite us to abandon the idea that police keep us all safe. Some of us trust or have trusted the police for a multitude of reasons: through fear, through lack of known 'alternatives', through wanting to believe that there is a way to be safe, much like when parents tell their children to dress or behave in certain ways, hoping this will prevent sexual violence and child abuse. These same parents, often survivors themselves, know on an atomic level that there is little correlation between what children do and the violence they are subjected to. Often these parental warnings in the shape of instructions and 'rules' are cloaked prayers, underneath it all nothing more than fingers crossed against a raging storm. Janey Starling described to me the 'psychological function' of police – that the mere desire for protection is what, for some people, maintains confidence in the police. In this sense, trust in the police is a form of optimism, a dream, something not pinned to reality. What would happen if we transformed that same optimism into trust in our communities, into our shared freedom dreams, and into ourselves?

The oscillating trajectory of mainstream feminism poses something between a cautionary tale and a millstone crushing forms of joy, tranquillity, contentment and connection that are possible by divesting from racial capitalism. As Alexis Pauline Gumbs writes, 'Trauma invades our dreams at night, our relationships, our health and our imaginations';[59] for this reason, healing is a foremost component of abolitionist futures. For reasons explored in the preceding chapters, the feminist imagination is characterised by a profound fragmentation: in some directions float fear, deficit and the unrelenting pursuit of 'the work' by any means necessary. This state of being cannot really be considered imaginative – more, it constitutes a co-option of imagination, in the way that clouds skating across the sun cloak us with chills that were inconceivable when sunbeams warmed our skin. Buffeted in other directions, but still part of the same wide sky, we continue to dream of different worlds, and of new and ancient ways of caring and cultivating. Many of the strategies we use to journey into freedom are already tried and tested; others have not yet even been dreamed of, and so the abolitionist feminist imagination is a precious resource we tend to. This fertile field will not produce delicate and vibrant ecosystems if we deny the potency of its existence – if we constantly and joylessly relegate our struggles to the field of pragmatism and disenchantment without surrender.

In order to dream we need to rest our heads and celebrate any efforts to take time away from the accumulation of capital: this is what Saidiya Hartman describes as 'the practices of refusal – shirking, idleness, and strike'.[60] Anti-capitalism in this sense involves the reclaiming of time as ours: as Rhiannon Firth and Andrew Robinson write, living in the urgent present under neo-liberalism places us in 'spatio-temporal closure' which results in our 'inability to imagine beyond present constructs of space and time'.[61] One of the most far-reaching shockwaves of racial capitalism is that we begin to believe that the way things are cannot be changed. Conversely, through healing practices, we rediscover the potential for shifts within us that we can carry out into the world. After all, in our dreams we can fly; our childhood toys morph into deep-sea creatures, and rooms have endless exit doors. The praxis of dreaming nudges us outside the enclosure of neoliberal time and space, and into wide forests, deep lagoons and endless possibilities for different worlds that are, in their varied and numerous components, already shimmering all around us.

Further Reading

Abercromby, Thomas, Roberts, Rosie and Thomas, Phil Crockett, eds. *The Moon Spins the Dead Prison: An Anthology of Abolition*. School of Abolition, 2022.

Abolitionist Futures. *Defund the Police: Reformist Reforms vs Abolitionist Steps for UK Policing*. Available at: abolitionistfutures.com/defund-the-police, 2020.

Cradle Community. *Brick by Brick: How We Build a World Without Prisons*. Hajar Press, 2021.

Day, Aviah Sarah and Octavia McBean, Shanice, *Abolition Revolution*. Pluto Press, 2022.

Duff, Koshka, ed. *Abolishing the Police*. Dog Section Press, 2021.

Elliott-Cooper, Adam. *Black Resistance to British Policing*. Manchester University Press, 2021.

Kenway, Emily. *The Truth about Modern Slavery*. Pluto Press, 2021.

Olufemi, Lola. *Feminism, Interrupted: Disrupting Power*. Pluto Press, 2020.

Quinlan, Hannah et al. *Disgrace: Feminism and the Political Right*. Arcadia Missa Publications, 2021.

Notes

Introduction

1. 'Jean Charles de Menezes' Cousin Wants Truth over "Smear" Stories', bbc.co.uk, 9 November 2020.
2. Emma Brazell, 'Sarah Everard's Killer Wayne Couzens Says He "Doesn't Deserve" Life in Prison', metro.co.uk, 5 May 2022.
3. Two of the survivors in this case brought a successful human rights claim against the police and were awarded compensation, despite then Home Secretary Theresa May attempting to block the case before it could reach the Supreme Court.
4. Jennifer McKiernan, 'Domestic Abuse: "The Police Didn't Believe Me … The Trauma Will Never Go Away"', bbc.co.uk, 25 November 2021.
5. Marienna Pope-Weidemann, 'The Police Failed My Cousin, Gaia Pope. Five Years on, Others like Her Are Still at Risk', theguardian.com, 15 July 2022.
6. Jennifer Brown, 'Policing in the UK', House of Commons Library, 29 September 2021.
7. Metropolitan Police, The Met's Direction: Our Strategy 2018–2025.
8. Beth Mann, 'More Britons Now Unconfident than Confident in the Police to Deal with Crime Locally', yougov.co.uk, 6 October 2021.
9. Cedric Robinson, *Black Marxism: The Making of the Black Radical Tradition*, Penguin Classics, 2021.
10. Anna Terwiel, 'What Is Carceral Feminism?', *Political Theory*, 48(4), 2019 DOI:10.1177/0090591719889946.

11. Fawcett Society, 'Fawcett Society Responds to Prime Minister's Comment on Misogyny as a Hate Crime' (press release), fawcettsociety.org.uk, 5 October 2021.

12. Ibid.

13. Elizabeth Bernstein, 'The Sexual Politics of the "New Abolitionism"', *Differences*, 18(3), 2007, DOI:10.1215/10407391-2007-013.

14. Centre for Women's Justice, End Violence against Women Coalition, Imkaan, and Rape Crisis England and Wales, 'The Decriminalisation of Rape: Why The Justice System Is Failing Rape Survivors and What Needs to Change', endviolenceagainstwomen.org.uk, November 2020.

15. Will Heath, '80% of Police Officers Time Spent Dealing with Non-crime', thejusticegap.com, 3 March 2020.

16. End Violence Against Women Coalition, 'Supreme Court Rules Police Failings in Worboys Breached Women's Human Rights', endviolence againstwomen.org.uk, 21 February 2018.

17. At Mayor's Question Time in March 2020, London mayor Sadiq Khan confirmed that new recruits to police forces in the UK are provided with 'unconscious bias' training. This is a widely disputed pseudoscientific framework which atomises experiences of racism to unconscious gut reactions and interpersonal clashes of 'bias', while leaving unchanged structures of inequality within organisations, as well as the institutions' actions towards external individuals and groups and those actions' legacies. In 2022, the College of Policing's 'Race Action Plan' set out its intention to increase trust in the police through introducing mandatory training on racism, anti-racism, Black history and its connection to policing.

18. Bernie O'Reilly, 'Policing for the Protection of Women', college.police .uk, 21 March 2021.

19. Women's Aid, 'Women's Aid Responded to the Joint Policing Report: A Duty to Protect', womensaid.org.uk, 24 August 2021.

20. SafeLives and Surviving Economic Abuse, 'Domestic Abuse Matters: Evaluation of Economic Abuse Training', survivingeconomicabuse.org.

21. Betsy Stanko and Katrin Hohl, 'Why Training Is Not Improving the Police Response to Sexual Violence against Women: A Glimpse into the "Black Box" of Police Training', in E. Milne, K. Brennan, N. South and J. Turton (eds), *Women and the Criminal Justice System: Failing Victims and Offenders?*, Palgrave Macmillan, 2018.

22. Ibid.

23. Joanna Taylor, 'Priti Patel Says "Majority" of Police Serve with "Utmost Integrity" in Wake of Sarah Everard Disappearance', independent.co.uk, 12 March 2021.

24. Tammy Hughes, 'Plain Clothes Officers "Will Not Be Deployed Alone" following Sarah Everard Case', standard.co.uk, 31 September 2021.

25. Home Office, definition of policing by consent (FOI release), gov.uk, 10 December 2012.

26. Home Office and the Rt Hon Karen Bradley MP, 'Coercive or Controlling Behaviour Now a Crime', gov.uk, 29 December 2015.

27. Department for Education and Lord Nash, 'Guidance on Promoting British Values in Schools Published' (press release), gov.uk, 27 November 2014.

28. Louise Ryan, '"Drunken Tans": Representations of Sex and Violence in the Anglo-Irish War (1919–21)', *Feminist Review*, 66, 2000, 73–94.

29. Tyler Krahe, 'A History of Violence: British Colonial Policing in Ireland and the Palestine Mandate', Graduate Theses, Dissertations, and Problem Reports, 2016.

30. Edna Mohamed, 'London's Metropolitan Police Face Criticism for Hosting Israeli Police Delegation', middleeasteye.net, 20 May 2022.

31. Avril Sharp, 'It's Time to Give Migrant Domestic Workers in the UK Their Rights Back', antislavery.org, 4 February 2021.

32. Kalayaan et al., 'Why the UK Must Reinstate the Original Overseas Domestic Worker Visa', briefing for report stage of the Nationality and Borders Bill in the House of Lords, kalayaan.org.uk, 1 March 2022.

33. Micha Frazer-Carroll, 'We Must Honour the Lives Lost at the Hands of Police', huckmag.com, 6 September 2021.

34. Jason Kornwitz, 'Here's How Police Violence Affects the Mental Health of Black People Aged 18 to 29', Boston College School of Social Work, 9 July 2021; see also S. Alang, C. VanHook, J. Judson, A. Ikiroma and P. B. Adkins-Jackson, 'Police Brutality, Heightened Vigilance, and the Mental Health of Black Adults', *Psychology of Violence*, 12(4), 2022, 211–20.

35. Lola Olufemi, *Feminism, Interrupted: Disrupting Power*, Pluto Press, 2020.

1. False Histories in the Shadow of the Empire

1. Sophie Lewis and Asa Seresin, 'Fascist Feminism: A Dialogue', *TSQ*, 9(3), 2022, 463–79.

2. K. Aune and R. Holyoak, 'Navigating the Third Wave: Contemporary UK Feminist Activists and "Third-Wave Feminism"', *Feminist Theory*, 19(2), 2017 DOI:10.1177/1464700117723593.

3. Leyla Reynolds, 'Rebecca Hall Is Uncovering the Hidden History of Women-Led Slave Revolts – and She's Doing It via Graphic Novel', gal-dem.com, 7 June 2021.

4. Curtis Jacobs, 'Catherine Flon', *Enslaved: Peoples of the Historical Slave Trade*, enslaved.org.

5. Aisha K. Finch, Cécile Fatiman and Petra Carabalí, 'Late Eighteenth-Century Haiti and Mid-Nineteenth-Century Cuba', in E. Ball, T. Seijas and T. Snyder (eds), *As If She Were Free: A Collective Biography of Women and Emancipation in the Americas*, Cambridge: Cambridge University Press, 2020, 293–311.

6. Judy Richardson, 'Slave Catchers, Slave Resisters', *Zinn Education Project*, zinnedproject.org.

7. M. Wollstonecraft and American Imprint Collection, *A Vindication of the Rights of Woman: With Strictures on Moral and Political Subjects*, Printed by William Gibbons, 1792.

8. Quoted in Ana Stevenson, 'Suffragettes and Slaves', *aeon*, aeon.co.

9. Quoted in Angela Y. Davis, *Women, Race and Class*, Vintage, 1983.

10. HL Deb 10 May 1922, vol. 50, col. 355.

11. Anon., *A Dialogue between a Well-Wisher and a Friend to the Slaves in the British Colonies by a Lady*, Bagster and Thomas, c.1828, p. 29.

12. Ruhi Khan, 'How White Feminists and Elites Appropriated Slavery, and Still Do', blogs.lse.ac.uk, 1 October 2020.

13. Jesse Daniels, 'Trouble with White Feminism: Racial Origins of US Feminism', racismreview.com, 18 February 2014.

14. Lori D. Ginzberg, *Elizabeth Cady Stanton: An American Life*, Hill & Wang, 2009.

15. Véronique Molinari, '"The Eugenic Vote": Eugenics and Suffrage Rhetoric in the Edwardian Period', in Véronique Molinari and Cyril Besson (eds), *Using and Abusing Science: Science and political discourse from Burke's "French Revolution" to Obama's Science Fair*, Cambridge Scholars Publishing, 2016, pp. 7–12.

16. Anne Taylor Allen, 'Feminism and Eugenics in Germany and Britain, 1900–1940: A Comparative Perspective', *German Studies Review*, 23(3), 2000, 477–505.

17. Christabel Pankhurst, *The Great Scourge and How to End It* (1913), Well-come Collection, closed stores K28515.

18. Stefan Anthony Slater, 'Containment: Managing Street Prostitution in London, 1918–1959', *Journal of British Studies*, 49(2) (April 2010), 332–57.

19. Ibid.

20. Eliza Riedi, 'Women, Gender, and the Promotion of Empire: The Victoria League, 1901–1914', *Historical Journal*, 45(3) (September 2002), 569–99.

21. Ibid.

22. Ibid.

23. Sarah Jackson, '"Women Quite Unknown": Working-Class Women in the Suffrage Movement', bl.uk, 6 February 2018.

24. 'The Story of the Co-operative Women's Guild', Co-operative Heritage Trust, 28 May 2020.

25. A letter from Eva Gore Booth and Esther Roper of the Lancashire and Cheshire Women Textile and other Workers' Representation Committee, *c.*24 October 1906, Manchester Central Library Archives, M50/2/1/230.

26. Vicky Iglikowski-Broad, Katie Fox and Rowena Hillel, 'Suffragettes, 1912: "rather broken windows than broken promises"', blog.nationalarchives. gov.uk, 9 March 2018; City of London Corporation, 'Suffragette bomb-ings', artsandculture.google.com.

27. Yvonne Eckersly, 'The Miners, Pit Brow Lasses and Women's Suffrage', *Past Forward*, 79 (August–November 2018).

28. Jacqueline Mulhallen, 'Sylvia Pankhurst and the Working Class Suf-fragettes', counterfire.org, 8 March 2018; see also Jacqueline Mulhallen, 'Women Workers of England', sylviapankhurst.com.

29. 'Unearthed Photograph Highlights Important Role of Indian Suffra-gettes', lse.ac.uk, 1 July 2019.

30. Ibid.; see also Ella Braidwood, 'The Queer, Disabled, and Women of Color Suffragettes History Forgot', vice.com, 5 February 2018.

31. Elizabeth Baker, 'Suffragette Palace: Sophia Duleep Singh (1876–1948), Hampton Court Palace and Votes for Women', in June Purvis and June Hannam (eds), *The British Women's Suffrage Campaign*, Routledge, 2020.

32. WSPU London branch secretary Eliza Adelaide Knight would later became a founding member of the Communist Party of Great Britain.

33. Jackson, 'Women Quite Unknown'.

34. As quoted in Sylvia Pankhurst, *The Suffragette Movement: An Intimate Account of Persons and Ideals*, Longmans, Green and Company, 1931.

35. Emmeline Pankhurst, 'Speech from the Dock', *Votes for Women*, 29 October 1908, 1.

36. Mulhallen, 'Sylvia Pankhurst and the Working Class Suffragettes'.

37. Joyce Marlow, *Suffragettes: The Fight for Votes for Women*, Virago, 2000.

38. Rosemary Hennessy and Chrys Ingraham, *Materialist Feminism: A Reader in Class, Difference, and Women's Lives*, Routledge, 1997.

39. The practice of prioritising material issues before turning to representational or symbolic ones has been an effective tactic throughout the history of social movements, from the Black Panther Party's breakfast clubs in the US to food parcels distributed to the families of striking British miners in the 1980s.

40. Nicoletta F. Gullace, 'The "White Feather Girls": Women's Militarism in the UK', openDemocracy.net, 30 June 2014.

41. Ibid.

42. The 'Allied powers' is a term used to describe the collection of countries led by the UK, France, Italy, Russia, Japan and, after 1917, the United States, who fought in the First World War against the coalition formed by Germany, Austria–Hungary, the Ottoman Empire and also Bulgaria after 1915.

43. 'Miss Pankhurst Chides Heckler: Lone German Sympathizer Quits Carnegie Hall Meeting in Disgust', *New York Tribune*, 25 October 1914, 9.

44. M. Allen, *The Pioneer Policewoman*, Chatto & Windus, 1925.

45. Alison Woodeson, 'The First Women Police: A Force for Equality or Infringement?', *Women's History Review*, 2(2), 1993, 217–32.

46. Nina Boyle, 'Women Volunteer Police', *The Vote*, 21 August 1914.

47. Woodeson, 'The First Women Police'.

48. International Centre for the History of Crime, Policing and Justice, 'The Women Police', open.ac.uk; see also John Carrier, *The Campaign for the Employment of Women as Police Officers*, Avebury, 1988.

49. Christabel Pankhurst, *c*.1908, transcript, British Library.

50. Alwyn Collinson, 'Vote for Women: The Groundbreaking Election of 1918', museumoflondon.org.uk, 14 December 2018.

51. Martin Pugh, 'Why Former Suffragettes Flocked to British Fascism', slate.com, 14 April 2017.

52. Rob Baker, *Beautiful Idiots and Brilliant Lunatics: A Sideways Look at Twentieth-Century London*, Amberley Publishing, 2015.

53. Mary Richardson, 'My Reply to Sylvia Pankhurst', *The Blackshirt*, 29 June 1934.

54. Angela McPherson, 'A Grandmother's Legacy: The Gift That Keeps on Giving?', *Women's History Review*, 30(4), 2021, 688–700.

55. Asa Seresin, 'Lesbian Fascism on TERF Island', 11 February 2021, asaseresin.com/2021/02/11/lesbian-fascism-on-terf-island.

56. Ann Taylor Allen, *Women in Twentieth-Century Europe*, Palgrave Macmillan, 2008; see also Ingrid Sharp and Matthew Stibbe, 'Women's International Activism during the Inter-war Period, 1919–1939', *Women's History Review*, 26(2), 2017, 163–72.

57. Aimé Césaire and Joan Pinkham, *Discourse on Colonialism*, NYU Press, 2000; see also Tanzil Chowdhury, 'From the Colony to the Metropole: Race, Policing and the Colonial Boomerang', in Koshka Duff, ed., *Abolishing the Police*, Dog Section Press, 2021.

58. Simin Fadaee, 'Bringing in the South: Towards a Global Paradigm for Social Movement Studies', *Interface*, 9(2), November–December 2017, 45–60.

59. 'History of Women's Struggle in South Africa', *South African History Online*, 21 March 2011.

60. Ibid.

61. Rozina Visram and Dr Chanda Mahal, 'Women in the Civil Disobedience Movements of the 1920s and 1930s', British Library, Voices of Partition, 7 November 2022.

62. Suruchi Thapar-Björkert, 'Gender, Nationalism and the Colonial Jail: A Study of Women Activists in Uttar Pradesh', *Women's History Review*, 1998, 7(4), 583–615.

63. Visram and Mahal, 'Women in the Civil Disobedience Movements of the 1920s and 1930s'.

64. Marissa Evans, 'Aba Women's Riots (November–December 1929)', blackpast.org, 27 March 2009.

65. George Padmore, *The Life and Struggles of Negro Toilers*, Red International of Labour Unions Magazine for the International Trade Union Committee of Negro Workers, 1931.

66. David M. Anderson, 'Stock Theft and Moral Economy in Colonial Kenya', *Africa*, 56, 1986, 399–416.

67. The campaign to abolish joint enterprise – Joint Enterprise Not Guilt by Association (JENGbA) – is predominantly organised by the mothers of boys who have been targeted by this legislation.

68. Ifeanyi-Ajufo, Nnenna, 'Gender, Anti-Colonialism and Nationalism: The Anti-Colonial Legacies of African Women', *Republic*, 8 September 2021.

69. W. Jilala and N. Lwoga, 'A Brief History of Forensic Services in Tanzania: Current Challenges and Mitigation Efforts', *Forensic Sci Int Synerg*, 9(4), April 2022, DOI: 10.1016/j.fsisyn.2022.100227.

70. Terence O. Ranger, *Dance and Society in Eastern Africa, 1890–1970: The Beni Ngoma*, University of California Press, 1975.

71. 'The Beni Dance', African Poems, africanpoems.net.

72. Tadasu Tsuruta, 'Popular Music, Sports, and Politics: A Development of Urban Cultural Movements in Dar Es Salaam, 1930s–1960s', *African Study Monographs*, 24(3), 2003, 195–222.

73. Albert Adu Boahen, ed., General History of Africa, vol. VII: Africa under Colonial Domination, 1880–1935, Heinemann, 1985.

74. 'Lessons from Three Women in the Vanguard of the Labour Movement (in Trinidad and Tobago)', Trinidad and Tobago Labour Media Project, 8 July 2012, lionhistorians.wordpress.com.

75. Anne S. Macpherson, *From Colony to Nation: Women Activists and the Gendering of Politics in Belize, 1912–1982*, University of Nebraska Press, 2007.

76. Adam Elliott-Cooper, *Black Resistance to British Policing*, Manchester University Press, 2021.

77. Following the labour rebellions, the British government sent a commission to the Caribbean to document living conditions, report on the causes of unrest and make recommendations for the future. The commission's findings (the Moyne report) detailed incredibly difficult living conditions and widespread poverty, and proposed reforms to social care and healthcare, agriculture, education and trade unionism in order to improve living standards. However, it also suggested that there was an inherent defective Caribbean character that had contributed to the country's impoverishment, recommending that 'an emergence of a spirit of self-help, thrift and independence' would be needed in order to steer the country into a better future.

78. Padmore, *How Britain Rules Africa*; see also Priyamvada Gopal, *Insurgent Empire: Anticolonial Resistance and British Dissent*, Verso, 2019.

79. C. J. Hogsbjerg, '"A Thorn in the Side of Great Britain": C. L. R. James and the Caribbean Labour Rebellions of the 1930s', *Small Axe: A Caribbean Journal of Criticism*, 15(2[35]), 2011, 24–42.

80. Quoted in Martin Pugh, *Women and the Women's Movement in Britain 1914–1959*, MacMillan, 1992.

81. '1957: Britons "Have Never Had It So Good"', bbc.co.uk.

82. Lemn Sissay, 'Young Caribbean Migrants and Growing Up in the UK', blackhistorymonth.org.uk, 21 August 2015; Kevin Searle, 'Before Notting Hill: Causeway Green and Britain's Anti-Black Hostel Riots', blog .nationalarchives.gov.uk, 22 June 2020.

83. Wilson Paul, 'The Development and Role of a Black Police Association in the Wider Police Modernisation Agenda', Metropolitan Black Police-man Association, September 2006.

84. Arsalan Samdani, 'The Brown in Black Power: Militant South Asian Organizing in Post-war Britain', *Jamhoor*, 3 (27 August 2019).

85. Lizzie B, 'Amy Ashwood Garvey (1897–1969)', *Women Who Meant Business*, 31 October 2021.

86. Stephen Brooke, 'Gender and Working Class Identity in Britain during the 1950s', *Journal of Social History*, 34(4), 2001, 773–95.

87. The 'angel in the house' is a literary trope (based on a mid-nineteenth-century poem by Coventry Patmore) used to describe the ideal Victorian housewife: a (white) woman who is meek, submissive and pious, and a devoted wife and mother.

88. Anne Alexander, 'Suez and the High Tide of Arab Nationalism', *International Socialism*, 2006.

89. Emily Cousins, 'Nottingham Riots (1958)', blackpast.org, 30 August 2010.

90. Colin Prescod, 'The "Rebel" History of the Grove', Institute of Race Relations, 6 June 2019.

2. A Symphony of Order and Chaos

1. *Burn Your Bra!*, featuring reporter Andy Price, 1968, BFI Player, from the collection of the South West Film and Television Archive (SWFTA).

2. Finn Mackay, 'Reclaiming Revolutionary Feminism', *Feminist Review*, no. 106, 2014, pp. 95–103.

3. George Stevenson, 'The Women's Liberation Movement and the Intracta-ble Problem of Class, *c.*1968–*c.*1979', Durham theses, Durham University, 2016.

4. Wilmette Brown, *Black Women and the Peace Movement*, Falling Wall Press, 1984.

5. HC Deb 23 April 1968, vol. 763, col. 61.

6. HC Deb 23 April 1968, vol. 763, col. 54.

7. Evan Smith and Marinella Marmo, 'Is There a Desirable Migrant? A Reflection on Human Rights Violations at the Border: The Case of "Virginity Testing"', *Alternative Law Journal*, 35(4), December 2010, 223–6.

8. 'Virginity Testing: Racism, Sexism, and British Immigration Control', imperialglobalexeter.com, 25 August 2014.

9. *Spare Rib* no. 81 (April 1979) quoted in 'Britain: Foreign Husbands and Virginity Test', *Isis International Bulletin*, 14, Summer 1980.

10. Sophia Siddiqui, '"Reclaiming Our Collective Past": Meeting Amrit Wilson', Institute of Race Relations, 8 November 2018.

11. 'Britain: Foreign Husbands and Virginity Test'.

12. Sundari Anitha and Sukhwant Dhaliwal, 'South Asian Feminisms in Britain: Traversing Gender, Race, Class and Religion', *Economic and Political Weekly*, 2019.

13. Beverley Bryan, Stella Dadzie and Suzanne Scafe, *The Heart of the Race: Black Women's Lives in Britain*, reprinted edn, Verso, 2018.

14. George Stevenson, T*he Women's Liberation Movement and the Politics of Class in Britain*, Bloomsbury, 2019.

15. Ibid.

16. 'How Ford's Striking Women Drove the Equal Pay Act', tuc.org.uk.

17. 'Today in London Radical History: Cleaners Win Strike in Ministry of Defence Buildings, 1972', pasttense.co.uk, 16 August 2016.

18. *Nightcleaners Part 1*, created by Berwick Street Film Collective, 1975, copyright Lux Artists' Moving Image.

19. Bryan et al., *The Heart of the Race*.

20. Ron Ramdin, 'The Imperial Typewriters Strike, 1974', libcom.org, 7 May 2016.

21. Ibid.

22. Bethan Bell and Shabnam Mahmood, 'Grunwick Dispute: What Did the "Strikers in Saris" Achieve?', bbc.co.uk, 10 September 2016.

23. Sundari Anitha, Ruth Pearson and Linda McDowell, 'From Grunwick to Gate Gourmet: South Asian Women's Industrial Activism and the Role of Trade Unions', *Revue française de civilisation britannique*, 23(1), 2018, DOI:10.4000/rfcb.1790.

24. Robert Reiner, 'Tony Bunyan, *The History and Practice of the Political Police in Britain*', *Crime and Social Justice*, 13, 1980, 55–8.

25. 'The Grunwick strike', *Working Class History* (podcast), episodes 67–8, August 2022; see also Jac St John, 'Rumours of "Rent-a-Mobs" and Miners Taking Over: The Policing of the Grunwick Strike', Special Branch Files Project, 4 March 2016, specialbranchfiles.uk.

26. Ibid.

27. Arsalan Samdani, 'The Brown in Black Power: Militant South Asian Organizing in Post-war Britain', *Jamhoor*, 3, 27 August 2019.

28. Niamh McIntyre, 'Funding for London's BME Refuges Slashed by Half in 7 Years', *Novara Media*, 2 October 2017.

29. Amina Mama, *The Hidden Struggle: Statutory and Voluntary Sector Responses to Violence against Black Women in the Home*, London Race and Housing Research Unit, 1989.

30. Kemi Alemoru, 'Meeting Mama Edwards, Manchester's Black Activist Hero', *gal-dem*, 31 October 2019.

31. Guru et al., 'Birmingham Black Sisters'.

32. Alemoru, 'Meeting Mama Edwards'; López de la Torre and Ana Laura, 'Manchester Black Women's Co-op', Remembering Olive Collective, 27 September 2007; Harmit Athwal and Jenny Bourne, 'Martha Osamor: Unsung Hero of Britain's Black Struggle', Institute of Race Relations, 17 November 2015.

33. Rowena Arshad and Mukami McCrum, 'Black Woman, White Scotland (a Comment on the Position of Black Women with Particular Reference to Scotland)', *Scottish Government Yearbook 1989*, ed. David McCrone and Alice Brown, Unit for the Study of Government in Scotland, University of Edinburgh; see also Francesca Sobande and layla-roxanne hill, *Black Oot Here: Black Lives in Scotland*, Bloomsbury, 2022, for more detail on the history of the WLM in Scotland.

34. 'Carolyn – Squatting in Brixton in the 1970s', *Do You Remember Olive Morris?*, Lambeth Archives, IV/279/2.

35. 'Liz Obi – Remembering Olive: Time to Pass the Memories On', *Do You Remember Olive Morris?*, Lambeth Archives, IV/279/2.

36. 'Black Parents Movement', George Padmore Institute, georgepadmore institute.org.

37. Fiona Rutherford, 'The Black Supplementary School Movement Is as Essential as It's Ever Been', *Black Ballad*, 13 December 2020.

39. Diane Reay and Heidi Safia Mirza, 'Uncovering Genealogies of the

Margins: Black Supplementary Schooling', *British Journal of Sociology of Education*, 18(4), 1997, 477.

39. Heidi Safia Mirza, '"The Golden Fleece": The Windrush Quest for Educational Desire', bl.uk, 4 October 2018.

40. Lucy Delap, 'Feminist Bookshops, Reading Cultures and the Women's Liberation Movement in Great Britain, *c.*1974–2000', *History Workshop Journal*, 81, 2016, 171–96.

41. Colin A. Beckles, '"We Shall Not Be Terrorized Out of Existence": The Political Legacy of England's Black Bookshops', *Journal of Black Studies*, 29(1), 1998, 51–72.

42. John Cunningham, 'Mangrove Four Sentenced', *Guardian*, 17 December 1971.

43. Robin Bunce and Paul Field, 'Thirteen Dead and Nothing Said', in Robin Bunce and Paul Field, *Darcus Howe: A Political Biography*, Bloomsbury Academic, 2014, 187–202, Bloomsbury Collections, Web, 7 Feb. 2023.

44. Ibid.

45. HC Deb 11 February 1981, vol. 998, col. 958

46. 'Spotlight on London's Radical Herstory: The Brixton Black Women's Group', pasttense.co.uk, 13 May 2020.

47. Tobi Thomas, 'Stella Dadzie, Feminist Pioneer: "The Black British Women's Movement Was About Life-And-Death Issues"', theguardian .com, 30 September 2021.

48. Ibid.

49. Anna E. Rogers, 'Feminist Consciousness-Raising in the 1970s and 1980s: West Yorkshire Women's Groups and Their Impact on Women's Lives', PhD thesis, University of Leeds, 2010.

50. 'Gail Lewis Discusses Brixton Black Women's Group', British Library, C1420/14, April 2011.

51. Kathie Sarachild, *Consciousness-Raising: A Radical Weapon*, ed. Cathy Brennan and republished by Organising for Women's Liberation, 25 September 2012; Rogers, 'Feminist Consciousness-Raising in the 1970s and 1980s'.

52. Bryan et al., *The Heart of the Race*.

53. Florence Binard, 'The British Women's Liberation Movement in the 1970s: Redefining the Personal and the Political', *Revue française de civilisation britannique* (online), 22 special edition, 2017, my emphasis.

54. Paula Akpan, 'The Anti-Black History of Contraception', yourdaye. com, 29 September 2023.

55. 'The Great Bluff That Led to a "Magical" Pill and a Sexual Revolution', *Fresh Air* (podcast), 7 October 2014.

56. P. V. Liao and J. Dollin, 'Half a Century of the Oral Contraceptive Pill: Historical Review and View to the Future', *Can Fam Physician*, 58(12), December 2012, e757–60.

57. J. Olszynko-Gryn, 'The Feminist Appropriation of Pregnancy Testing in 1970s Britain', *Womens Hist Rev*, 28(6), July 2017, 869–94.

58. 'OWAAD Introductory Talk: Black Women in Britain', Organisation of Women of Asian and African Descent (OWAAD), March 1979, Black Cultural Archives.

59. Judith A.M. Scully, 'Black Women and the Development of International Reproductive Health Norms', in J. Levitt, ed., *Black Women and International Law: Deliberate Interactions, Movements and Actions*, Cambridge University Press, 2015, 225–49.

60. Bryan, *The Heart of the Race*. 149.

61. Guru et al., 'Birmingham Black Sisters'.

62. It's not evidenced whether advocates of self-examination engaged with the history of the speculum itself. The invention of the device is commonly attributed to Dr Marion Sims, who developed gynaecological surgical methods on enslaved Black women prior to the invention of anaesthetic, and later on working-class Irish women patients in the mid-1800s, which raises questions around the issue of consent, bodily autonomy and intellectual property regarding 'his' medical developments.

63. 'The Feelings Behind the Slogans Part 4', producer/director Lizzie Thynne, British Library.

64. *Women and Their Bodies*, Boston Women's Health Book Collective, 1970.

65. 'Talking about gender', troubleandstrife.org.

66. Ibid.

67. 'Redstockings Manifesto', 7 July 1969, republished on historyisaweapon.com, my emphasis.

68. Judith Weinraub, 'Germaine Greer: Opinions That May Shock the Faithful', *New York Times*, 22 March 1971.

69. Germaine Greer, *The Female Eunuch*, HarperCollins Publishers Inc., 2008.

70. 'Spotlight on London's radical herstory'.

71. Margaretta Jolly, *Sisterhood and After: An Oral History of the UK Women's Liberation Movement*, Oxford University Press, 2021, 182 (emphasis in original).

72. Helena Kennedy, *Misjustice: How British Law Is Failing Women*, Vintage Publishing, 2019.

73. Helen Pidd and Alexandra Topping, '"It Was Toxic": How Sexism Threw Police Off the Trail of the Yorkshire Ripper', theguardian.com, 13 November 2020.

74. 'Remembering Reclaim the Night, 1977', ayewellhmm.wordpress.com.

75. Finn Mackay, 'Mapping the Routes: An Exploration of Charges of Racism Made against the 1970s UK Reclaim the Night Marches', *Women's Studies International Forum*, 44, 2014, 46–54.

76. Steve Rose, '"She Was Not a Woman to Back Down": The Fearless Black Campaigner Who Helped to Scrap the UK's "Sus" Law', theguardian .com, 2 December 2022; Joseph Maggs, 'Fighting Sus! Then and Now', Institute of Race Relations, 4 April 2019.

77. Natalie Thomlinson, 'The Colour of Feminism: White Feminists and Race in the Women's Liberation Movement', *History*, 97(32), 2012, 453.

78. Ibid.

79. Hazel V. Carby, 'White Woman Listen! Black Feminism and the Boundaries of Sisterhood', in Mirza, *Black British Feminism*, 49.

80. Guru et al., 'Birmingham Black Sisters', 196–214.

81. Valerie Amos and Pratibha Parmar, 'Challenging Imperial Feminism', *Feminist Review*, 17, 1984, 3–19.

82. Ibid., 57.

83. Amos, Valerie, and Pratibha Parmar, 'Challenging Imperial Feminism', *Feminist Review*, 80, 2005, 49.

84. Thomlinson, 'The Colour of Feminism', 190.

85. Erika Rackley and Rosemary Auchmuty, eds, *Women's Legal Landmarks: Celebrating the History of Women and Law in the UK and Ireland*, Hart Publishing, 2019.

86. Jo Freeman, 'The Tyranny of Structurelessness', jofreeman.com.

87. 'Jane Hutt', bl.uk, Sisterhood and After collection.

88. Carmen, Gail, Shaila and Pratibha, 'Becoming Visible: Black Lesbian Discussions', *Feminist Review*, 17, 1984, 54.

89. 'Spotlight on London's Radical Herstory'.

90. Paula Akpan, 'Gal Wine: The Secret History of Sistermatic', crack magazine.net, 20 March 2023.

91. 'Spotlight on London's Radical Herstory'.

92. Salma Al-Hassan, 'Black Women Organising: What We Can Learn from the Rise and Fall of OWAAD', uomhistory.com, 1 October 2020.

93. 'Black Women Organising: Brixton Black Women's Group', libcom.org, 17 April 2017.

94. Gayatri Thanki, Swati Patel and B.L., 'DUH-soundscapes-5: Tales and Reminiscences', part of the Department of Unruly Histories by Meera Shakti Osborne, cubittartists.org.uk.

95. 'London Rebel Dykes of the 1980s', lgbtplushistorymonth.co.uk, 2 December 2014.

96. K. Plummer, 'The Lesbian and Gay Movement in Britain: Schisms, Solidarities and Social Worlds', in Barry D. Adam, Jan Willem Duyvendak and André Krouwel, eds, *The Global Emergence of Gay and Lesbian Politics: National Imprints of a Worldwide Movement*, Temple University Press, 1999, 133–57.

97. Julie Bindel, 'My sexual revolution', theguardian.com, 30 January 2009.

98. Carmen et al., 'Becoming visible'.

99. Leeds Revolutionary Feminist Group, *Love Your Enemy? The Debate between Heterosexual Feminism and Political Lesbianism*, Onlywomen Press, 1981.

100. Carmen et al., 'Becoming Visible', 61.

101. Bec Wonders, '"Please Say More": Mediating Conflict through Letter-Writing in British Second Wave Feminist Periodicals, 1970–1990', PhD thesis, Glasgow School of Art, published on Repository of Art Design Architecture Research (RADAR), 2021.

102. 'Stella Dadzie Discusses OWAAD', bl.uk, Sisterhood and After Collection, 2011.

103. Amina Mama, *Beyond the Masks: Race, Gender and Subjectivity*, Routledge, 1995, 4.

104. 'Black Women Organising: Brixton Black Women's Group', libcom.org.

105. Bryan et al., *The Heart of the Race*.

106. Tracy Fisher, 'Black Women, Politics, Nationalism and Community in London', *Small Axe*, 6(1), 2002, 133–50.

107. 'Spotlight on London's Radical Herstory'.

108. Jaimee A. Swift, 'On the Power of Stella Dadzie: A Radical Pioneer of the Black Women's Movement in Britain,' blackwomenradicals.com.

109. Bryan et al., *The Heart of the Race*.

110. Guru et al., 'Birmingham Black Sisters'.

3. The 'Sectorification' of Radical Struggle

1. 'The Opening of the First Refuge' (1971), womenslegallandmarks.com, 8 August 2017.
2. Carol Dix, 'Hell from Home', theguardian.com, 16 October 1975.
3. Ibid.
4. Zora Simic, 'From Battered Wives to Domestic Violence: The Transnational Circulation of Chiswick Women's Aid and Erin Pizzey's *Scream Quietly or the Neighbours Will Hear* (1974)', *Australian Historical Studies*, 51(2), 2020, 107–26.
5. Mama, *The Hidden Struggle*, 270.
6. Ibid., 271.
7. Ibid.
8. Erika Rackley and Rosemary Auchmuty, eds, *Women's Legal Landmarks: Celebrating the History of Women and Law in the UK and Ireland*, Hart Publishing, 2019.
9. 'The Opening of the First Refuge'.
10. Rackley and Auchmuty, Women's Legal Landmarks.
11. Angela Davis, *Women, Race and Class*, Random House, 1981, 198.
12. Susan Brownmiller, *Against Our Will: Men, Women and Rape*, Simon and Schuster, 1975.
13. Alison Diduck. 'First Rape Crisis Centre, 1976', in Erika Rackley and Rosemary Auchmuty, eds, *Women's Legal Landmarks: Celebrating the History of Women and Law in the UK and Ireland*, Hart Publishing, 2019.
14. Ian Blair, *Investigating Rape: A New Approach for Police*, Croom Helm, 1985.
15. Ibid.
16. Ibid.
17. Bianca Fileborn and Rachel Loney-Howes, *#MeToo and the Politics of Social Change*, Palgrave Macmillan, 2019.
18. Sophie Beatrice June Pike, 'A Critical Exploration of Changes to the Investigation of Homicide in England and Wales from the 1980s to the Present Day', PhD thesis, University of South Wales/Prifysgol De Cymru, available on pure.southwales.ac.uk, 2018.
19. Conservative general election manifesto, 1979, Thatcher Archive, available at margaretthatcher.org.
20. Colin Yeo, 'Briefing: What Is the "Right of Abode" in UK Immigration and Nationality Law?', freemovement.org.uk, 18 September 2019.

21. Jenny Douglas, 'Black Women's Activism and Organisation in Public Health: Struggles and Strategies for Better Health and Wellbeing', *Caribbean Review of Gender Studies*, 13, 2019, 56.

22. Ibid.

23. Mustafa Dikeç, *Urban Rage: The Revolt of the Excluded*, Yale University Press, 2017.

24. 'Elaine Bowes: The Evolution of Black and Minority Ethnic Housing Associations', elimhousing.co.uk.

25. Kate Murray, 'Black Housing Bodies Helped Build Communities', theguardian.com, 8 December 2010.

26. 'Remarks on Orgreave Picketing ("Attempt to Substitute the Rule of the Mob for the Rule of Law")', Thatcher Archive, available at margaret thatcher.org.

27. Diarmaid Kelliher, 'Solidarity, Class and Labour Agency: Mapping Networks of Support between London and the Coalfields during the 1984–5 Miners' Strike', PhD thesis, University of Glasgow, available at core. ac.uk, 2017.

28. Quoted in ibid.

29. Ian Gough, 'Thatcherism and the Welfare State: Britain Is Experiencing the Most Far-Reaching Experiment in "New Right" Politics in the Western World', *Marxism Today*, 1980, 12.

30. Bryan et al., *The Heart of the Race*, 179.

31. Speech to Scottish Conservative conference, Thatcher Archive, available at margaretthatcher.org.

32. Jerry White, 'The Greater London Council 1965 to 1986', in Ben Kochan, ed., *London Government: 50 Years of Debate: The Contribution of LSE's Greater London Group*, London School of Economics and Political Science, 2008, 6–9.

33. Michael Jacobs, 'Farewell to Greater London Council', *Economic and Political Weekly*, 21(30), 1986, 1306–8.

34. Sue Lieberman, 'Women's Committees in Scotland', *Scottish Government Yearbook 1989*, Paul Harris Publishing, 1989, 246.

35. Sally Weale, 'Beyond Red Ken', theguardian.com, 20 December 1999.

36. Vic Parsons. 'Lesbian Activist Linda Bellos Went to the Supreme Court to Back Trump Administration during Landmark LGBT Cases', *Pink News*, 9 October 2019; 'Clear spot: 17th December 2015 (the GLC story)' (podcast), hosted by K. Biswas on Resonance FM, available on mixcloud .com.

37. Carmen et al., 'Becoming Visible'.

38. Lieberman, 'Women's Committees in Scotland', 261.

39. Joyce Gelb, *Feminism and Politics: A Comparative Perspective*, University of California Press, 1989; see also Joni Lovenduski and Vicky Randall, *Contemporary Feminist Politics: Women and Power in Britain*, Oxford University Press, 1993.

40. I. Bruegel and H. Kean, 'The Moment of Municipal Feminism: Gender and Class in 1980s Local Government', *Critical Social Policy*, 15 (44–5), 1995, 147–69.

41. Donatella Della Porta and Mario Diani, *Social Movements: An Introduction*, 2nd edn, Blackwell, 2006, 20.

42. Freya Johnson Ross, 'Professional Feminists: Challenging Local Government Inside Out', *Gender Work Organ*, 26, 2019, 521.

43. Ibid.

44. 'Series 4: A Woman's Place (AWP)', Glasgow Women's Library Archive, GB 1534 CLCBLG/4.

45. 'Former Jagonari Women's Centre, 183–185 Whitechapel Road', surveyoflondon.org, 17 April 2018.

46. Lucy Collins, 'We All Know an Abused Woman, although We May Not Realise It', *WI Life*, April 2014, 21

47. Guru et al., 'Birmingham Black Sisters'.

48. In issue 19 of radical feminist magazine *Trouble and Strife*, a BBWG member notes, 'In the end it was agreed that we would [seek external funding], but Olive (Morris) also insisted that she be statemented as saying she did not want to be a part of this, based on a political analysis of the state getting involved in the lives of Black people and buying them off.'

49. 'Spotlight on London's Radical Herstory'.

50. Bryan et al., *The Heart of the Race*, 179.

51. 'Opening Statement on Behalf of Suresh Grover and the Monitoring Group', Undercover Policing Enquiry, 10 November 2020, available at ucpi.org.uk.

52. Bryan et al., *The Heart of the Race*, 259.

53. Ibid.

54. Quoted in Jenny Turner, 'Dark Emotions', *London Review of Books*, 24 September 2020.

55. Bryan et al., *The Heart of the Race*, 264.

56. Arundhati Roy, *The End of Imagination*, Haymarket Books, 2016.

57. Rachel Loney-Howes, *Online Anti-rape Activism: Exploring the Politics of the Personal in the Age of Digital Media*, Emerald Studies in Criminology, Feminism and Social Change, Emerald Publishing Limited, 2020, 24.

58. Jane W. Grant, 'Governance, Continuity and Change in the Organised Women's Movement', PhD thesis, University of Kent, 2001.

59. 'History', at victimsupport.org.uk.

60. Alison Diduck. 'First Rape Crisis Centre, 1976'.

61. Rackley and Auchmuty, *Women's Legal Landmarks*.

62. Jacobs, 'Farewell to Greater London Council'.

63. John Cunningham, 'From the Archive, 1 April 1986: Thatcher Abolishes the GLC', theguardian.com, 1 April 2014.

64. Emil Horton, Philip Tew and Leigh Wilson, *The 1980s: A Decade of Contemporary British Fiction*, Bloomsbury Academic, 2017.

65. Lucy Brownson, 'Radical Objects: The London Women's Handbook', historyworkshop.org.uk, 5 May 2022.

66. Amrit Wilson, 'Why Feminists Should Support the Struggle for Prison and Police Abolition', *OpenDemocracy*, 22 July 2020.

67. Adam Forrest, 'Margaret Thatcher Refused to Warn People against "Risky Sex" in Aids Campaign, Says Former Tory Minister', independent .co.uk, 8 February 2021.

68. Hugo Young, 'Margaret Thatcher Left a Dark Legacy That Has Still Not Disappeared', theguardian.com, 8 April 2013.

69. Benjamin Bowling, Robert Reiner and James W. E. Sheptycki, *The Politics of the Police*, Oxford University Press, 2019.

70. 'Self-defence and the Prevention of Crime', cps.gov.uk, 9 September 2022.

71. Robert Booth and Matthew Taylor, 'G4S Guards Found Not Guilty of Manslaughter of Jimmy Mubenga', theguardian.com, 16 December 2014.

72. Barak Ariel, Matthew Bland and Alex Sutherland, '"Lowering the Threshold of Effective Deterrence" – Testing the Effect of Private Security Agents in Public Spaces on Crime: A Randomized Controlled Trial in a Mass Transit System', *PLoS ONE*, 12(12), 2017, e0187392; see also McLaughlin and Murji's study of 'postmodern' policing, Eugene McLaughlin and Karim Murji, 'The Postmodern Condition of the Police', *Liverpool Law Review*, 21 1999, 217–40.

73. See timeline at spycops.co.uk.

74. McLaughlin and Murji, 'The Postmodern Condition of the Police'.

75. Camille Kumar, 'Feminism Then and Now', *feminists@law*, 4(1), 2014, 4.

76. Clare Wiper, 'Feminist Anti-Violence Activism in Austerity Britain: A North East of England Case Study', doctoral thesis, Northumbria University, 2018; see also 'Multi-Agency Risk Assessment Conference (Marac) Guidance for GPs', safelives.org.uk, 2016.

77. Evie Muir, 'How Can We End Gendered Violence, when the Violence Against Women and Girls Sector Is Violent?', gal-dem.com, 9 June 2022.

78. Anitha and Dhaliwal, 'South Asian Feminisms in Britain'.

79. Grant, 'Governance, Continuity and Change', 136.

80. 'Gender-based Violence Workers', uvwunion.org.uk.

81. Grant, 'Governance, Continuity and Change', 203.

82. Helena Kennedy, Foreword, Rahila Gupta, ed., *From Homebreakers to Jailbreakers: Southall Black Sisters*, Zed Books, 2003.

83. Wendy Larcombe, 'Falling Rape Conviction Rates: (Some) Feminist Aims and Measures for Rape Law', *Feminist Legal Studies*, 19, 2011, 29.

84. C. McGlynn, 'Feminist Activism and Rape Law Reform in England and Wales: A Sisyphean Struggle?', in C. McGlynn and V. Munro, eds, *Rethinking Rape Law: International and Comparative Perspectives*, Routledge, 2010, 139–53.

85. Heidi Safia Mirza, and Yasmin Gunaratnam, "'The Branch on Which I Sit': Reflections on Black British Feminism, *Feminist Review*, no. 108, 2014, 125–33.

86. Jacinda Swanson, 'Self Help: Clinton, Blair and the Politics of Personal Responsibility', *Radical Philosophy*, 101, 2000, p.29.

87. Mama, *Beyond the Masks*, 13.

4. Feminisms of Fear and Resistance in the New Millennium

1. 'A Choice by Right: A Report on the Working Group on Forced Marriage', Home Office Communications Directorate, June 2000.

2. 'Written Evidence from Southall Black Sisters (ASB 32)', publications.parliament.uk, 20 June 2013.

3. 'Forced Marriage: A Consultation Summary of Responses', Home Office, June 2012.

4. Lis Bates and Marianne Hester, 'No Longer a Civil Matter? The Design and Use of Protection Orders for Domestic Violence in England and Wales', *Journal of Social Welfare and Family Law*, 42(2), 2020, 136.

5. Ibid.

6. Liz Kelly et al., *Evaluation of the Pilot of Domestic Violence Protection Orders*, Research Report 76, Home Office, November 2013.

7. Ania Moroz and Alex Mayes, 'Learnings from the London Domestic Violence Protection Order Caseworker Project', Victim Support, May 2019; see also 'Transforming the Response to Domestic Abuse Consultation', womensaid.org.uk, May 2018.

8. 'Domestic Abuse Protection Notices/Orders Factsheet', Home Office, 11 July 2022.

9. 'G4S PLC', investigate.afsc.org/company/g4s.

10. 'Serco Agrees to Repay £68.5m after Tagging Scandal', bbc.co.uk, 19 December 2013.

11. Alexandra Topping, 'Police and CPS Scrap Digital Data Extraction Forms for Rape Cases', theguardian.com, 16 July 2020.

12. By 2020 this spending would be slashed by 84 per cent.

13. 'Female Genital Mutilation: Question for Home Office', parliament.uk, 2 March 2020.

14. 'Forced Marriage Consultation Document', gov.uk, 9 August 2021.

15. Gina Martin, 'Was I a Poster Girl for Carceral Feminism?', shado-mag .com, 16 February 2022.

16. Catharine A. MacKinnon, 'Where #MeToo Came from, and Where It's Going', *Atlantic*, 24 March 2019.

17. HC Deb 22 June 2022, vol. 512, col. 167.

18. *Intersecting Inequalities: The Impact of Austerity on Black and Minority Ethnic Women in the UK*, report by Women's Budget Group, Runnymede Trust, RECLAIM & Coventry Women's Voices, wbg.org.uk, 10 October 2017.

19. Ibid.

20. Niamh McIntyre, 'Funding for London's BME Refuges Slashed by Half in 7 years', novaramedia.com, 2 October 2017.

21. 'The State of the Sector: Contextualising the Current Experiences of BME Ending Violence against Women and Girls Organisations. An Executive Summary', *Imkaan*, imkaan.org.uk, 2015.

22. Anjum Mouj, 'A Right to Exist: A Paper Looking at the Eradication of Specialist Services to BAMER Women and Children Fleeing Violence', imkaan.org.uk, 2008; 'Call to End Violence against Women and Girls: Action Plan', HM Government, homeoffice.gov.uk, March 2011.

23. Lucy Hadley, 'Refuge Services Toolkit', dahalliance.org.uk, 2019.

24. 'Rape and Sexual Abuse in Yarl's Wood Immigration Removal Centre 2005–2015', womenagainstrape.net, 2015.

25. 'A History of Immigration Detention in the UK (1914–2018): Resource from Refugee History and Right to Remain', righttoremain.org.uk, 2018.

26. A. Phipps, 'White Tears, White Rage: Victimhood and (as) Violence in Mainstream Feminism', *European Journal of Cultural Studies*, 24(1), 2021, 85.

27. Helena Spector, 'We Need a Bill That Doesn't Leave Migrant Women Behind', thejusticegap.com, 22 January 2019.

28. 'The Domestic Abuse Act', solacewomensaid.org.

29. bell hooks, *Feminist Theory: From Margin to Center*, South End Press, 1984. p.88.

30. 'Policing "More Politicised" Says Dame Cressida', policeprofessional. com, 9 March 2022.

31. Deborah Joseph, '"I do consider myself a feminist", Priti Patel Tells GLAMOUR, as She Announces FGM Campaigner Nimco Ali as an Independent Government Advisor for Tackling Violence against Women and Girls', glamourmagazine.co.uk, 9 October 2020.

32. See Emily Kenway's critique of research conducted by Liz Kelly and Linda Regan in Emily Kenway, *The Truth about Modern Slavery*, Pluto Press, 2021.

33. *Strengthening the Law on Domestic Abuse: Impact Assessment*, Home Office, 28 November 2014.

34. 'Poor Housing Conditions Contributes to Asylum Seekers' Marginalisation in the UK', ucl.ac.uk, 21 June 2022.

35. Ending Violence against Women and Girls Strategy 2016–2020, HM Government, March 2016.

36. 'Open Letter Opposing the Nordic Model', decrimnow.org.uk, April 2021.

37. As quoted in Niki Seth-Smith, 'What Is "Femonationalism"?', open democracy.net, 13 July 2017.

38. *No Silence to Violence: A Report on Violence against Women in Prostitution in the UK*, Sex Worker Advocacy and Resistance Movement (SWARM), 17 December 2018.

39. Sam Matthews, 'Women and Prevent: Perceptions, Policy and Encounter', PhD thesis, University of Lincoln, available at eprints.lincoln.ac.uk, December 2020.

40. Anitha and Dhaliwal, 'South Asian Feminisms in Britain', 17.

41. Lucy Ward, 'Cherie Blair Pleads for Afghan Women', theguardian.com, 20 November 2001.

42. Wilson, 'Why Feminists Should Support the Struggle for Prison and Police Abolition'.

43. Abeera Khan, 'The Violence of Essentialism', *Religion and Gender*, 11(1), 2021, p.101.

44. 'West Midlands Police: Serve and Protect with Cloud', accenture.com, 2020.

45. 'Kent Police Cancel "Predictive Policing" Software', softwaretesting news.co.uk.

46. *PredPol Operational Review: Initial Findings*, by Kent police, published by statewatch.org.

47. 'Review of the Metropolitan Police Service Gangs Violence Matrix: A One-Year Update', Mayor of London Office for Policing and Crime, london.gov.uk, January 2021.

48. James Ball and Symeon Brown, 'Why BlackBerry Messenger Was Rioters' Communication Method of Choice', theguardian.com, 7 December 2011.

49. Radhika Sanghani, 'A Day in the Life of the Everyday Sexism Hashtag', telegraph.co.uk, 15 April 2015.

50. Fiona Vera-Gray, Clare McGlynn, Ibad Kureshi and Kate Butterby, 'Sexual Violence as a Sexual Script in Mainstream Online Pornography', *British Journal of Criminology*, 61(5), 2021, 1243–60.

51. Julie Bindel, 'Joanna Yeates Murder: Legislation Needed on Incitement to Gender Hatred', theguardian.com, 28 October 2011.

52. Biological essentialism is the idea that there are particular aspects of human experience (behaviours, abilities and interests) that are predetermined by our biology, and are not influenced and guided by social expectations and norms. This plays into the idea of an inherent gender division, suggesting that men are intrinsically logical, and that women are intrinsically more caring and loving, for example.

53. Linda Stupart, 'On Trauma, Paranoia, and Fascism (and on Nina Power)', thewhitepube.co.uk, 4 May 2019.

54. Ibid.

55. Sara Maria De-Benedictis, Shani Orgad and Catherine Rottenberg, '#MeToo, Popular Feminism and the News: A Content Analysis of UK Newspaper Coverage', *European Journal of Cultural Studies*, 22(5–6), 2019, 718–38.

56. Nicola Slawson, 'Katie Ghose: "Risky Proposals Are Coming on Top of Cuts That Led Many Refuges to Close"', theguardian.com, 13 March 2018.

57. Jess Phillips, 'Jess Phillips: I Just Want Women to be Safe', harpersbazaar.com, 12 March 2021, my emphasis.

58. Black Lives Matter UK (@ukblm), 18 October 2017.

59. Bianca Fileborn and Rachel Loney-Howes, *#MeToo and the Politics of Social Change*, Palgrave Macmillan, 2019, 26.

60. Nadine Hartmann, 'Telling What We Don't Know: Confession, Varité, #MeToo', *European Journal of Psychoanalysis*, October 2022, journal-psychoanalysis.eu.

61. Alison Phipps, 'White Tears, White Rage: Victimhood and (as) Violence in Mainstream Feminism', *European Journal of Cultural Studies*, 24(1), 2021, DOI:10.1177/1367549420985852.

62. Stuart Hall, 'Race, Articulation and Societies Structured in Dominance', in Colette Guillaumin and Marion O'Callaghan, eds, *Sociological Theories: Race and Colonialism*, UNESCO, 1980, 341.

63. Diyora Shadijanova and editors, 'Reclaim These Streets' Girl Boss Feminism Will Never Set Us Free', gal-dem.com, 15 March 2021.

64. '"Police Are the Perpetrators": Sisters Uncut Set to Take Action One Year on from Clapham Common Vigil', sistersuncut.org, 7 March 2022.

5. Defund, Abolish, Now

1. Hari Ziyad, 'What Do We Do with Abusers like R. Kelly if We Abolish Prisons?', blackyouthproject.com, 8 January 2019.

2. J. Fleetwood and J. Lea, 'Defunding the Police in the UK: Critical Questions and Practical Suggestions', *Howard Journal of Crime and Justice*, 61(2), 2022, 167–84.

3. 'Police Funding for England and Wales: User Guide', Home Office, 28 July 2023.

4. *Policing for a Better Britain: Report of the Independent Police Commission*, available at statewatch.org.

5. Laura Bainbridge, 'Police and Crime Commissioners: New Agents of Crime and Justice Policy Transfer?', *Policing and Society*, 31(6), 2021, 721–34.

6. Richard Garside, 'The End of an Undemocratic Experiment?', Centre

for Crime and Justice Studies, 27 November 2013.

7. Lizzie Dearden, 'Elected Police and Crime Commissioners Can Be "Absolutely Bleeding Hopeless", Report Told', independent.co.uk, 14 September 2018.

8. HL Deb 21 December 2022, vol. 826, col. 1140.

9. 'Police Funding', politics.co.uk.

10. M. McElhone, Tom Kemp, Sarah Lamble and J. M. Moore, 'Defund – Not Defend – the Police: A Response to Fleetwood and Lea', *Howard Journal of Crime and Justice*, 62, 2023, 277–82.

11. 'Recruitment of 20,000 New Police Officers to Begin "within Weeks"', bbc.co.uk, 26 July 2019.

12. 'Police Funding for England and Wales 2015 to 2023', Home Office, 12 July 2022.

13. Angel Parker, 'What about the Rapists and Murderers?', medium.com, 24 June 2020.

14. 'The Nature of Violent Crime in England and Wales: Year Ending March 2022', ons.gov.uk, 9 November 2022.

15. 'Key Findings from Analysis of Domestic Homicide Reviews: October 2019 to September 2020', Home Office, 12 April 2023.

16. 'Prison Abolition Part 1: The Serial Killer Question', habeasquaestus .com, 2 March 2016.

17. Ibid.

18. Richard Howard and Conor Duggan, 'The Epidemiology of Antisocial Personality Disorder', in *Antisocial Personality: Theory, Research, Treatment*, Cambridge University Press, 2022, 71–87.

19. 'Life Sentences', sentencingcouncil.org.uk.

20. 'Investigation and Prosecution of Rape: Eighth Report of Session 2021– 22', Home Affairs Committee, available at publications.parliament.uk, 12 April 2022.

21. Ibid.

22. Sam Francis, 'Sexual Assaults by Prisoners Treble since 2010', bbc.co.uk, 16 October 2018.

23. Tim Newburn, '"Tough on Crime": Penal Policy in England and Wales', *Crime and Justice*, 36(1), 2007, 425–70.

24. Nadia Whittome, 'Tory Neglect of Child Asylum Seekers Was a Choice, Not Some Disastrous Mistake', labourlist.org, 3 February 2023.

25. Cassandra Mensah, 'If We Abolish Police, What Happens to Rapists?', *Teen Vogue*, 24 June 2020.

26. Jared Knowles and Andrea J. Ritchie, 'Cops Don't Stop Violence: Combating Narratives Used to Defend Police Instead of Defunding Them', available at defundpolice.org, July 2021.

27. Ibid.

28. Duff, *Abolishing the Police*.

29. Mia Mingus, 'Pods and Pod Mapping Worksheet', Bay Area Transformative Justice Collective, June 2016.

30. Aviva Stahl, 'We Have Already Stopped Calling the Cops', bustle.com, 21 July 2020.

31. Brit Dawson, 'It's Time to Abolish the Family', huckmag.com, 5 October 2022.

32. Ireti A. Adegbesan, 'Bodily Autonomy of Young Children: Mothers' Perspectives of Appropriate Acceptance or Rejection of Affection for Their Toddler and Preschool-Aged Children', PhD thesis, University of North Carolina at Greensboro, 2021, available at NC Digital Online Collection of Knowledge and Scholarship.

33. Richie Reseda (@richiereseda), carousel of text-based images reflecting on the conviction of Tony Lanez, Instagram, 24 December 2022.

34. Vikram Dodd and Sarah Haque, '80% of UK Police Accused of Domestic Abuse Kept Jobs, Figures Show', theguardian.com, 17 March 2022.

35. 'Police Perpetrated Domestic Abuse: Report on the Centre for Women's Justice Super-Complaint', hmicfrs.justiceinspectorates.gov.uk, 30 June 2022.

36. Imkaan and UN Women, *A Thousand Ways to Solve our Problems: An Analysis of Existing Violence Against Women and Girls (VAWG) Approaches for Minoritized Women and Girls in the Western Balkans and Turkey*, 2018.

37. Neha Kagal, '"In the Union I Found Myself": The Impact of Collectivization of Informal Economy Women Workers on Gender Relations within the Home', PhD thesis, SOAS University of London, 2017.

38. Mia Mingus, 'Transformative Justice: A Brief Description', leaving evidence.wordpress.com, 9 January 2019.

39. Melanie Brazzell, 'Theorizing Transformative Justice: Comparing Carceral and Abolitionist Selves, Agencies, and Responsibilities', Koshka Duff, ed., *Abolishing the Police*, 2021, 166.

40. Catherine Walker and Cathy Pharoah, 'Foundation giving trends 2021', acf.org.uk, December 2021.

41. Fahid Qurashi, 'The Prevent Strategy and the UK "War on Terror": Embedding Infrastructures of Surveillance in Muslim Communities', *Palgrave Communications*, 4(1), 2018, 1–13.

42. 'Local Delivery Best Practice Catalogue: Prevent strategy. Office for Security and Counter Terrorism. Home Office', Home Office, 2015, available at powerbase.info.

43. Laura J. Shepherd, 'White Feminism and the Governance of Violent Extremism', *Critical Studies on Terrorism*, 15(3), 2022, 727–49.

44. Paula X. Rojas, 'Are the Cops in Our Heads and Hearts?', *The Revolution Will Not be Funded: Beyond the Non-Profit Industrial Complex*, Duke University Press, 2017. p.205.

45. Ruth Wilson Gilmore, 'The Worrying State of the Anti-Prison Movement', socialjusticejournal.org, 23 February 2015.

46. Rojas, 'Are the Cops in Our Heads and Hearts?', 207.

47. INCITE! Women of Color against Violence, *The Revolution Will Not Be Funded: Beyond the Non-profit Industrial Complex*, Duke University Press, 2017.

48. 'How we ran a mutual aid fund: SWARM's Covid-19 pandemic response', SWARM, August 2020.

49. Marina Bell, 'Abolition: A New Paradigm for Reform', *Law and Social Inquiry*, 46(1), February 2021, 32–68, 42.

50. Reflecting on their poetic work *Zong!*, which is composed using words of a court report on the murder of Africans on board an eighteenth-century slave ship, M. NourbeSe Philip told Dzifa Benson, 'we breathe now for those people who could not breathe.' Dzifa Benson, 'Breath and Space: M NourbeSe Philip Interviewed by Dzifa Benson', poetrysociety .org.uk.

51. bell hooks, *Outlaw Culture: Resisting Representations*, Routledge, 2006, 248.

52. Sarah Lamble, 'Practising Everyday Abolition', Ed. Koshka Duff, *Abolishing the Police*, Dog Section Press, 2021, 148.

53. Robin Wall Kimmerer, *Braiding Sweetgrass: Indigenous Wisdom, Scientific Knowledge, and the Teachings of Plants*, Penguin, 2020, 111.

54. Lori L. Heise, 'Violence against Women: An Integrated, Ecological Framework', *Violence against Women*, 4(3), 1998, 262–83.

55. Antonio Gramsci, *The Gramsci Reader: Selected Readings 1916–1935*, ed. David Forgacs, New York University Press, 2000, 423.

56. bell hooks, *Outlaw Culture: Resisting Representations*, Routledge, 2006, 248.

57. Quoted in 'Abolition Journal: If You're New to Abolition: Study Group Guide', anarchistagency.com, 30 June 2020.

58. Vikram Dodd, 'Tackle Poverty and Inequality to Reduce Crime, Says Police Chief', theguardian.com, 18 April 2021.

59. CR10 Publications Collective, *Abolition Now! Ten Years of Strategy and Struggle against the Prison Industrial Complex*, AK Press, 2008, 167.

60. Catherine Damman, 'Saidiya Hartman on Insurgent Histories and the Abolitionist Imaginary', artforum.com, 14 July 2020.

61. Rhiannon Firth and Rhiannon Robinson, 'For a Revival of Feminist Consciousness-Raising: Horizontal Transformation of Epistemologies and Transgression of Neoliberal TimeSpace', *Gender and Education*, 28(3), 2016, 343–58.